W·I·N·E·M·A·K·I·N·G
M·O·N·T·H B·Y M·O·N·T·H

OTHER BOOKS BY BRIAN LEVERETT

Home Beermaking
Instant Winemaking
Basic Winemaking
Basic Preservemaking
Home Brewing (Editor)
Winemaking from Kits
The Home Cellar (in preparation)

W·I·N·E·M·A·K·I·N·G
M·O·N·T·H
B·Y
M·O·N·T·H

Brian Leverett

PRISM PRESS
Bridport, Dorset · San Leandro, California

Originally published in 1979.
This revised edition published in 1986 by
PRISM PRESS
Bridport, Dorset DT6 3NQ
Great Britain
and in the U.S.A. by
PRISM PRESS
P.O. Box 778
San Leandro CA 94577
United States of America

Distributed in Australia by
Book & Film Services
P.O. Box 226
Artarmon N.S.W. 2064

Distributed in Canada by
Raincoast Book Distribution
112 East 2nd Avenue
Vancouver B.C. V5T 1C8

Distributed in New Zealand by
Roulston Greene Publishing Associates Ltd.
Unit 14, 46 Ellice Road,
Auckland 9

Distributed in the U.S.A. by
Interbook Inc.
Suite 370, 14895 East 14th Street
San Leandro, CA 94577

ISBN Hardback 0 907061 78 8
ISBN Paperback 0 907061 77 X

Made and printed in Great Britain by the
Guernsey Press Co. Ltd., Guernsey, Channel Islands.

C·O·N·T·E·N·T·S

Introduction, legal position, equipment

Sugar, the role of air in fermentation, acidity, nutrients, temperature

Planning your own recipes, the hydrometer, strength of wines, tannin, body, flavour and bouquet

Extraction and sterilising of the must, the hot method, the cold method, clarification, starting the wine, the main types of wine.

Sterilising equipment, making the wine, the no chemical method

Standard recipes for making wines from all the main ingredients

Table of approximate alcohol strength, maturation period and types of wine produced from the recipes.

Recipes for wines from all parts of the world, how to make wines from ingredients not covered in the standard recipes, wines from canned fruits, fruit juices and grape juice concentrates.

Blending, maturation, serving and cooking with wine, correcting faults, exhibiting wines.

A·U·T·H·O·R'·S F·O·R·E·W·O·R·D

As soon as sugar rationing ended in the fifties I was sent to collect elderberries for winemaking and the fascination with the hobby, which has lasted for over a quarter of a century, began.

Winemaking has undergone a tremendous change since my early days, when there were few recipes and virtually no equipment available. Wine was simply made by floating a piece of yeast-covered toast on the liquid contained in an earthenware pot. It was the high incidence of failure with this method and the ever growing interest that led to innovation. New methods, ingredients and equipment were enthusiastically tried. The best became part of the accepted practice, whilst the others have disappeared from the winemaking scene.

As a result, today it is possible to make a wide range of wine, both of the traditional country type and those similar to commercials, with only the occasional disappointment.

But from lecturing and from receiving mail as a writer on winemaking, I became aware that many people are still making fundamental mistakes. This, coupled with the constant demand for recipes, indicated a demand for a book that dealt with all aspects of winemaking in a manner that everybody could understand.

Moreover the time is right for a rethink on winemaking. Many professionals have rejected the traditional methods completely; discarding free ingredients and replacing them with expensive alternatives. Above all much of the fun seems to go out of the hobby when we forget that the day out in the country, to collect the fruit, is as exciting as the drinking of the wine.

But for the best results we must use the best of the modern techniques.

My technique therefore combines the best of the old and the new methods. Wherever possible I have also tried to suggest ways to economise. Winemaking should not be expensive otherwise one of the main aims is lost.

The recipes and methods given are the result of several years experimentation, during which time I experienced several failures. If some particular aspects, such as sterilisation and special precautions with ingredients are stressed, it is to ensure that you do not experience the disappointments of my early days.

Really this is two books in one, the first consisting of instructions on how to make wines and recipes; the second is concerned with simplified theory (and how it can be applied). A detailed knowledge of chemistry will not make you a good winemaker, only a little care and attention will do that.

I have attempted to include all the information a winemaker might require, including a critical discussion of alternative methods which will enable you, if you wish, to adjust your recipes and alter your technique, knowing in advance that your wine is going to be up to the required standard.

Some ingredients do make better wines than others, and since if you look hard enough you can find recipes for virtually every non poisonous plant, the beginner making only a few gallons needs to know which wines to make. Rather than just give a recipe I have in many instances expressed my own opinion of the wine. I have also included, for what I believe to be the first time, a table giving a star rating to each of the main wines described, their approximate alcohol level and the minimum and optimum maturation times. For completion's sake I also decided to include, with suitable warnings, recipes for ingredients that although often used do not make good wines.

The recipes are arranged month by month so that at any particular time of the year you have several to choose from.

Contrary to general opinion there is a correct time to start winemaking TODAY.

Brian Leverett, Poole, Dorset

I·N·T·R·O·D·U·C·T·I·O·N

No aspect of self-sufficiency has quite as many advantages as making your own wine. The cost savings are considerable, for a very modest outlay you can have a full drinks cabinet, enjoy wines every day, and keep alive a traditional country craft whose origins are lost in the mists of antiquity. Very little space is required; the flat lends itself as readily as the farmhouse to winemaking; the time involved is minimal, but when you produce really good wine, the sense of achievement is as great as with any hobby.

In recent years few activities have enjoyed such a rapid resurgence of popularity as home winemaking and most families have at some time attempted to make the odd gallon or two. In some cases odd being the operative word. At their best country wines are excellent, and once you have acquired the taste (a process which takes virtually no time at all), making and drinking wines becomes part of your way of life.

Many would-be winemakers have been put off the hobby by tasting wines that were far from enjoyable, whilst others have tried to make wines and have stopped when their initial efforts were little better. Such wines are the result of bad technique — it is important to follow meticulously a few simple rules, the most important of which is hygiene throughout — or of poor recipes. Unless you use the correct ingredients in the right amounts you will never make a balanced wine.

THE LEGAL POSITION

Some confusion exists as to the legal position with regards to winemaking. You may make as much wine as you wish for your own and your friends' consumption. But it is illegal to sell wine without a special licence — details of which may be obtained from the Customs and Excise — nor can you raffle it or dispose of it in any way for gain, even if the money goes to charity.

The romance of cheating the exciseman, by distilling homemade alcohol, will always appeal to some. But not only is this practice illegal, it is extremely dangerous. Distillation results in the build up of lethal poisons, as well as increasing the alcohol concentration and should under no circumstances be attempted by the amateur.

It is also illegal to attempt to increase the alcohol concentration by freezing some of the water out of a wine in a refrigerator. Whilst the laws are generally similar in many other parts of the World, if you are in any doubt check with the authorities before making the wine.

EQUIPMENT

Unlike most hobbies very little expense is involved when you start winemaking. The beginner is advised to buy only the essentials at first, avoiding expensive kits and many of the pieces of equipment that have been developed for the pastime. As your knowledge and interest increase you may wish to try filters, scientific test kits and some of the range of chemicals that are now available from home brew centres that have sprung up in nearly all towns. But to begin with you need buy very little in the way of equipment, most of the requirements you will already possess in your kitchen. However some of the new materials such as enzymes and special winemaking yeasts, which cost very little and add a minimal amount to the price of a gallon of wine, make our task so much easier and result in a wine of a far superior quality, that to ignore them represents a false economy.

You will need two white plastic buckets, one for starting the wine in and a second for transferring to. Under no circumstances use a metal bucket — never allow wine or the ingredients it is made from to come into direct contact with metal, except for stainless steel saucepans that may be used for boiling fruit — as the acids in the wine dissolve some of the metal which is probably a cumulative poison. It is also thought that some of the colourings used in plastics may be poisonous and for this reason only white plastic is recommended.

Special fermentation buckets with airtight fitted lids are best for the purpose, and you will need to buy these if you make several gallons, but initially you may improvise by covering the top of any suitable bucket with a layer of plastic self-adhesive film. This material has a wide range of uses in winemaking, because although it acts as a seal and will not allow air to enter the wine, if the pressure in a container builds up as a result of the carbon dioxide generated by fermentation, the excess gas can escape. On other occasions when the pressure above the wine is equal to that of the atmosphere, gas will not pass through the barrier.

Do not cover buckets with pieces of cloth, wood or metal trays. All of these allow germ-carrying air to enter the must — the fermenting liquid — very easily.

The most expensive items that you will need to buy are demijohns, the vessels in which the wine is fermented. You will need one for every gallon of wine that you are making. Some economies can be made by using brown glass demijohns, which are cheaper and far less popular than clear glass. This is surprising, but they are far better because they filter out much of the light which causes deterioration and loss of colour of wines fermented in daylight. Equally suitable for fermentation are the non-returnable one gallon whisky bottles used in many public houses and clubs, which landlords are often only too willing to give away.

The way to minimise the number of demijohns that you require is to bottle the wine as soon as fermentation is complete. It is usually recommended that wine is stored in bulk but the advantages of this, other than convenience, are probably exaggerated.

You may, when you have decided which wines you prefer to make, wish to ferment them in five gallon batches. It takes only a little more effort to make five gallons than one. With five gallons you have enough to drink during the year it is made and still have some over that can be left to mature. However, it

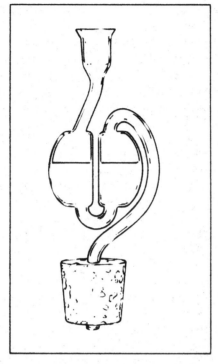

an airlock

is not advisable to make five gallon batches until you have made a particular wine once or twice and know that you really enjoy it.

Five gallon fermenting vessels, carbuoys, are extremely expensive, but most off-licences will sell you sherry fives. These are plastic containers which draught sherry is stored in. Although not rigid in themselves, if kept in the cardboard containers that are supplied with them, they are ideal for our purpose. If these are not available, you can with a little ingenuity make your fermenting vessels from a whole range of plastic containers. Once fermentation has ceased, transfer the wine to bottles as it will not mature satisfactorily in plastic.

Another type of container that should not be used for maturing wine is small wooden barrels, whilst being aesthetically pleasing they are almost impossible to sterilise. Wines stored in them almost invariably become infected and they are best ignored by the amateur except for decoration.

One item that you must buy is air locks. Do not be tempted to use cotton wool plugs as they are not impervious to germs. Whilst all airlocks are efficient in that they allow the carbon dioxide generated by the wine to escape and stop the entry of airborne infections, the short stubby type are better than the old fashioned taller design, which tend to get knocked over if several demijohns are stored together. Buy plastic rather than glass, which if it breaks is extremely dangerous.

Most airlocks depend upon a water seal to function, and since at the temperature at which fermentation is conducted they tend to dry out quickly, it is necessary to check the level regularly. For a few pence more you can overcome the problem by buying the dry valve type airlock, which functions just as efficiently wet or dry. The valve may be covered with water so that you can observe the escape of carbon dioxide and follow the progress of fermentation if you wish, but it will continue to protect the wine should you forget to top up the level after evaporation.

The airlocks must be fitted into a rubber bung, under no circumstances use a cork as these are porous and do not give an airtight fit. If you use a sherry five, unscrew the top cap and push out the middle section, containing the tap, from the cap. Place the bung and airlock into the vacant space in the cap and screw back into position.

The only other piece of equipment that you will need to buy is a racking tube. Again there are several designs to choose from, but the simplest (and cheapest) is the best, it is also the easiest to sterilise. Racking tubes are constant sources of infection unless you are careful. Buy or make a racking tube consisting of a U-bend about half an inch (1.25 cm) long on one side and a foot (30 cm) on the other, with about six feet (2 metres) of transparent plastic attached to the large end. Equally simple and effective are the T-junction racking tubes. Do not use rubber tubing as it is impossible to see if the equipment is clean and it tends to give a rubbery taste to the wine.

To make certain types of wine it is necessary to buy a hydrometer. These are both cheap and easy to use, but you can make most kinds of wine without one simply by following the recipes.

You will already have the rest of the equipment you need in your kitchen, such as colanders, potato masher, large plastic spoons and measuring jugs. Winemaking like most country crafts benefits from a little ingenuity. An effective strainer may be made by placing a piece of muslin two layers thick in a colander on top of a bucket. Providing the muslin is sterilised by boiling, it may be used several times without replacement.

Should you find yourself in the fortunate position of possessing more fruit than you have equipment to deal with it — a common occurrence during September — store it in a deep freeze. This is done by selecting sound fruit, ruthlessly discarding any showing signs of decay, and placing it in plastic bags. Squeeze out any excess air, fasten the bag and place in the freezer. Most soft fruits will keep for a year this way, and are better for winemaking, as the small ice crystals formed help to break up the fruit and release more juice than fresh fruit.

With just a few pieces of equipment, the contents of the kitchen and a little imagination you are ready to make your first gallon of wine.

F·E·R·M·E·N·T·A·T·I·O·N

To be a winemaker rather than somebody who just makes wine, it is necessary to understand fermentation, the process by which fruit juices are converted into wine, in order to appreciate why certain operations are important and to avoid expensive wastage.

The production of wine involves several complex processes, many of which have still not been fully investigated, but the manufacture of alcohol and all other important aspects to the country winemaker are fully understood.

It is the simple plant, yeast, that converts the liquid into wine by feeding on sugar, liberating alcohol and carbon dioxide from it in the process. The alcohol then reacts with the acids present to produce compounds, termed esters, that completely change the character of the liquid. The taste becomes different from that of the fruit from which it was made, and the wine develops its own unique bouquet and flavour. (Only wines that are very young or are made from strongly flavoured fruit retain much of the original flavour of that fruit. Instead they develop a character of their own.) The most important characteristic developed by a wine is vinosity and this will only occur if the must contains grapes, for this reason amongst others, grapes in the form of sultanas, raisins or either concentrated or natural juices are included in most recipes.

SUGAR

Costly confusion exists as to which sugar is preferred for the task. The yeast releases complex chemicals, enzymes, that first invert the sugar. The term inversion of sugar is derived from the original method of classifying sugars. Household sugar, sucrose, turns polarised light to the right but after the action of the yeast the products glucose and fructose turn the same light to the left. Because of this inversion of the light the mixture of glucose and fructose is known as invert sugar. It is possible to buy invert sugar, but as this is far more expensive and since the yeast performs the process in about twenty four hours, a mere moment in the overall time taken to make the wine, the extra expense cannot be justified. Demerara sugar has a completely different flavour from that of household sugar, which in some cases improves the wine and should always be used where specified in a recipe, but never in other cases, because what adds to that character of one wine, detracts from that of another. Sugar candy and lump sugar have both been suggested for wine making, but these only involve extra work to make the same quality wine. Honey is a mixture of sugars, but it is the esters which go to make up the bouquet of the flowers from which it was gathered that are responsible for the flavour of mead. A mild honey is an ideal ingredient, but it should not be used to replace sugar in recipes other than mead, melomel, cyser or pyment as the flavours may interact and produce a wine that is neither one thing nor the other.

Both the carbon dioxide and the alcohol liberated by the yeast during fermentation poison it and will ultimately kill it. The carbon dioxide usually presents no problems to the winemaker as it escapes from the precious liquid, a process that can be greatly helped by gently agitating the wine — either by stirring whilst in the bucket or gently shaking the demijohn. This forces the gas out of the solution and should be performed daily at the start of the fermentation when the rate of production is at the highest and weekly thereafter until all activity ceases. With the gradual build up of alcohol the yeast will begin to lose its activity until, at the concentration of sixteen per cent, the yeast finally dies. This is the highest alcohol level obtainable in a drink without distilling the liquid. Even this degree of alcohol will not be obtained unless you take care to use a suitable wine yeast and feed the plant. Up to about twelve per cent alcohol, the average strength of commercial table wines, can be reached without any special effort; it is the final four per cent that presents the problems. If too much sugar is incorporated in the must, or it is not completely dissolved before the yeast is added, it will dehydrate the yeast by osmosis and kill it: the same mechanism is employed when beans are preserved in salt. If you are attempting to make a high alcohol wine, this problem can be overcome by adding the sugar in two batches, the initial amount when the juice is prepared and the remainder when this has fermented out. The cessation of bubbles escaping from the air lock does not necessarily mean that the wine has finished working. The wine may have stuck for a variety of reasons, all resulting from bad wine making. This should present no problems if you follow the instructions, but it is good practice always to check that the wine is dry before adding extra sugar. This can be done either scientifically with a hydrometer, or by tasting a sample to ascertain if there is any residual sweetness. The good wine maker misses no opportunity to sample his brews.

YEAST

There are several types of yeast on the market and whilst it is possible to make wine with all of them, some are more suitable than others.

Bakers Yeast

Originally all country wines were made from bakers yeast but its main disadvantage is that it originated from breweries where selected strains have been evolved to produce top quality beers. Beers have a far lower alcohol content than wines and the tolerance of the yeast to alcohol is far less than that of a true wine yeast. Consequently they tend to stop fermenting earlier and make poorly flavoured, weak drinks. Bakers yeasts are therefore not favoured for wine making. However, they do tend to start working far earlier than other yeasts and are ideal for cider making.

General Purpose Yeast

These are specially dried; they quickly regain their activity when placed in a suitable environment such as a wine must. General purpose wine yeasts, which are the best yeasts for winemaking, can be bought in sachets to make one batch of wine or in small drums containing sufficient yeast to make several gallons. Although they do not keep indefinitely, they do retain their activity for several months if stored in a cool dry place. So decide whether you intend making several gallons or just the occasional brew before buying your yeast.

Specialised Yeast

One recent innovation of wine making has been the marketing of yeast strains similar to those used to make the finest commercial wines in the world. Of course these are more expensive and unless used with grapes, or for one of their special properties such as temperature or alcohol tolerance, they hold virtually no advantage for the country wine maker. A commonly held misconception is that if you provide a certain strain of yeast, irrespective of the ingredients, the finished wine will bear a strong resemblance to a desired commercial type. This is not true, ingredients have a far greater influence on wine type than the yeast. Specialised yeast may be bought either in the dried form or as a culture in a suitable liquid medium. There is little to choose between either type.

Whichever type of yeast you choose it will be inactive. Due to the variable shelf life and the need to start fermentation as quickly as possible it used to be best to allow the yeast to regain much of its activity before adding to the must. The layer of carbon dioxide that formed on top of the liquid could therefore quickly start offering protection from attack by air-borne spoilage yeast. This was done by starting a small scale fermentation in a bottle forty eight hours before it was needed. The keener interest has lead to a quicker turnover of yeast, which is today far more reliable and there is no need to use a starter bottle, except in those instances where the musts have been treated with Campden tablets. For the average winemaker, who has only limited time to spend on the activity, wines are best made by adding half a teaspoonful of dried yeast straight to the must.

You are unlikely to experience any of the problems which are usually exaggerated by writers not prepared to deviate from standard procedures, providing you know the yeast to be fresh; the must is fully sterilised and placed in a bucket with an airtight lid, which is only good winemaking practise.

THE ROLE OF AIR IN FERMENTATION

The small quantity of yeast added to a gallon of must, about half a teaspoonful, is itself insufficient to ferment the liquid and must be allowed to breed. This stage is preceded by the lag phase, which, depending upon the temperature, lasts from twelve to forty eight hours, during which period the dried yeast takes up moisture and nutrients and increases in size. The end of this period is heralded by the first escape of bubbles, the sign that the wine making process has begun!

For rapid breeding to occur the yeast must have access to a large quantity of air. The process termed aerobic fermentation results in the production of a large number of yeast cells and is the most active stage in the yeast's cycle.

Aerobic fermentation is accompanied by a voluminous head as a result of the large quantities of carbon dioxide generated and will, depending upon the temperature, take from four days to a fortnight to subside. During this stage the wine must be kept covered, but sufficient space should be allowed to ensure that adequate air is present. As a rule only half fill the container with liquid. If you transfer too quickly to a demijohn, the head will continue to develop and bubble up through the air lock. It is equally important though to ensure that the liquid is placed into a demijohn as soon as the head has subsided, otherwise the wine will start to oxidise. Oxidation is a term that describes several different processes that involve the addition of oxygen to the compounds present in the wine. Such reactions can not occur in the presence of large amounts of carbon dioxide, as soon as the carbon dioxide level decreases after aerobic fermentation the wine is open not only to biological but also chemical attack. Oxidation can result in a wine becoming discoloured in the same way that an apple is if it is cut and allowed to stand in the air. As well as giving an undesirable colour this causes some of the alcohol to be converted into acetaldehyde.

This compound gives sherry its characteristic taste and whilst it is essential in this type of wine, and special methods are given in the recipe to ensure its development, it detracts from the flavour of all other wines and every precaution should be taken to ensure that it is omitted. Another reason for not allowing aerobic fermentation to proceed after the initial head has subsided, is that under these conditions the efficient conversion of sugar to alcohol does not occur, most of the sugar being converted to carbon dioxide. Oxygen is chemically combined in sugar and it is only when the yeast cannot get its requirements from the air that it takes it all from sugar, producing maximum alcohol in the process. In all cases (except in making sherry when the amount of air allowed to come in contact with the wine must be carefully controlled) after the initial fermentation has taken place all air must be excluded from the wine.

If the initial fermentation is carried out in the presence of the fruit, it is important that the liquid should not be kept in the presence of the fruit for more than the specified time. Many substances that the fruit contains are not soluble in water, but readily dissolve in the newly formed alcohol. One of these compounds, tannin, is particularly important. If the initial fermentation is too short, insufficient tannin is extracted and the wine is bland. But a far worse danger is that if too much tannin is extracted as a result of over exposure of the fruit to alcohol, the resulting wine will be so harsh that you will not be able to drink it for several years. It is only those wines with excessive tannin that take many years to mature.

Since it is the yeast that is going to convert the liquid into wine, it is common sense to provide the plant with ideal conditions. Once sufficient air has been provided to bring the colony up to strength, and there is enough sugar present to yield the required alcohol level, the yeast has three other requirements, the correct level of acidity, the right nutrients and a suitable temperature.

ACIDITY

The question of acidity in winemaking is extremely complicated and the home winemaker is advised to use only one acid, citric, in the compounding of his must. There are people, whose sole aim seems to be ensuring that wine making is as complicated as possible, who advocate using a mixture of different acids. But there are more important factors in the overall flavour of the finished wine than the acid type involved, and since the bulk of ingredients are so far removed from the grape, on which these mixtures are based, there is little to be gained by using anything other than citric acid. If fruit is the main ingredient, depending upon the type, it will provide part and in some cases all of the necessary acid. Extra acid, it is sometimes suggested, should be provided in the form of lemons. Apart from the extra cost and work involved in liquidising the fruit, you have a far greater degree of control over the amount of acid if you add citric acid powder, the main acid ingredient of lemons, than the fruit itself which will contain different amounts of acid depending upon its size. One method of providing a wine with sufficient acid is to replace 1 teaspoon of citric acid with a half pound (250 gm) can of gooseberries. As well as the acid a certain amount of body, flavour and sugar are obtained. These appear to be in perfect balance, the extra sugar results in more alcohol being formed which the wine can now carry and overall this ingredient appears to improve most wines, where extra acid is required. If you choose to include this in any of the recipes, I have omitted this ingredient to simplify the procedure and to keep the costs as low as is consistent with producing a good wine, add the fruit and juice with the other fruit.

Do not worry about the different acidity that occurs from year to year in the fruit that you use. The balance of all wines allows for a slight variation in the acidity. If there is a slight, deficiency of acid in the finished wine (and this is all that seasonal variations will produce), then extra can always be added. If there is a slight excess then this will mellow with keeping. But unless there is a certain minimum acid level at the start of fermentation the yeast will not be able to survive and the wine will have a bitter or even medicinal taste.

NUTRIENTS

Being a plant, yeast has certain nutritional requirements and whilst it may be possible to satisfy partially these from the fruit without any help from you, a little fertiliser in the form of winemaking nutrients can be bought very cheaply and should be used according to the maker's instructions. There is very little, if any, financial advantage to be gained from making your own nutrient but should you be unable to obtain a suitable supply then simply add half a teaspoonful of a mixture, obtained by combining seven parts ammonium phosphate and three parts magnesium sulphate (Epsom salts), to each gallon of wine. When buying your chemicals for winemaking check that they are tested to B.P. standard in order to ensure that they are suitable for use as additives. In addition to these compounds, you should also add a 12 mg tablet of vitamin B_1 (thiamin).

TEMPERATURE

The importance of temperature to good wine making cannot be over emphasised. Whilst yeast can stay alive, going into a stage of virtual hibernation, at temperatures below freezing and probably not be killed until well in excess of 100°F (38°C), the temperature range for top quality winemaking is far more restrictive. Below 65°F (18°C) fermentation is far too slow whilst above 75°F (23°C), unless special yeasts are used, off flavours develop from decaying dead yeast cells, and many of the esters that are responsible for the bouquet and flavour are lost. The optimum to produce a top quality wine in a reasonable period of time is 70°F (21°C). All the time scales in the recipes are quoted on the basis that this is the temperature at which fermentation is conducted. Even a difference of a few degrees will greatly affect the time taken for certain stages to be reached. Do not let this deter you from wine making. If the initial head does not subside, or fermentation is not complete in the time specified, it is probably due to incorrect temperature; so just wait and watch until it is complete before proceeding to the next stage.

There are many different ways of providing the correct temperature, fermenting in the airing cupboard or even next to a central heating radiator being the most popular. But it is important to ensure that the temperature is constant. If it is allowed to drop, then the yeast will lose most of its activity. This is not too serious during the early stages as the plant soon recovers when the temperature rises again. As the alcohol concentration rises, the yeast will be far less tolerant of it and will experience greater difficulty in regaining its activity and, as a result, fermentation may prematurely cease.

With a little ingenuity it is possible to solve the temperature problem in most houses, but if you intend making several batches of wine, it is best to make a fermentation cabinet.

FERMENTATION CABINET

This should consist of a box 15 inches × 15 inches (40 cm × 40 cm) to hold four demijohns, or one 21 inches × 21 inches (55 cm × 55 cm) to hold six, and you are strongly recommended to make the larger since you will find you require more and more space as your interest grows.

The box may be fitted with either front opening doors, or a fitted hinged lid. Bore a hole through the side of the box to take an electrical flex. Connect this first to a thermostat that can be set to 70°F (21°C) and then to a small electrical heater, those designed for aquariums are ideal for the purpose. The running costs of such fermentation cabinets are not high, but to make them even cheaper line the inside of the cabinet with insulation material, such as fire-proof expanded tiles. To minimise heat losses by radiation, cover the tiles with a layer of metallic baking foil. To the side of one of the cabinet walls, hang a thermometer to check the temperature. Fermentation temperatures refer to the air surrounding the demijohns, not that of the liquid itself which will be far higher, as a result of the heat produced by the chemical production of carbon dioxide. During the early stages, when the yeast is most active and you are providing a temperature of 70°F (21°C) the liquid itself may well be as high as 85°F (29°C).

For those people who do not wish to make their own fermentation cabinet, and it really is quite easy, there are several different devices for maintaining temperature during fermentation.

The simplest to use are heating mantles on which the demijohns are placed. These work on the principle that the yeast remains at the bottom of the container and if that region is kept warm, then fermentation will proceed. With heating mantles it is particularly important that they are used in a room which itself is heated and free from draughts, as they only boost the temperature by a set amount. If an insulated cover is made, then the efficiency is greatly increased. The occasional winemaker, or the person who is about to make his first brew, may utilise the heat generated by the fermenting yeast, simply by lagging the container. A demijohn which has several layers of newspaper taped to it, will, in a moderately warm room, retain sufficient heat to allow the fermentation to continue without interruption.

In the tropical and semi-tropical regions of America and Australia, the problem is the reverse of that normally encountered in the temperate zones, namely ensuring that the temperature is not too high.

Here it is essential to find a cool part of the house where the temperature does not exceed 75°F (24°C) as a maximum — lower if possible — at any time of the day. This maximum can be extended by 5°F (2.5°C) if you use a Tokay yeast.

If fermentation has to be conducted at this higher temperature all stages in the wine making process will be completed sooner. Rather than rely on my guide to when the initial fermentation is complete, look for the cessation of rapid activity, after three or four days, and strain into a demijohn immediately. Ensure also that the wine is racked immediately any sediment appears to avoid the accelerated decomposition of the lees, which produces a musty taste and renders the wine undrinkable.

Testing the tolerance of Tokay yeast to temperature, I once succeeded in fermenting a wine at 95°F (35°C) to approximately 14% alcohol in eight days. It tasted terrible.

By ensuring that you cater for the yeast's few basic requirements you will be rewarded with better wines ready for drinking in a shorter space of time.

I·N·G·R·E·D·I·E·N·T·S

By choosing different types of grapes, grown in different regions of the world and using various fermentation techniques, commercial winemakers produce from one fruit every type of wine that can be bought. Our ingredients in general are certainly not as versatile as the grape which alone has the right sugar, acid, tannin and other compounds to produce the many different types of wine available. But by adjusting the relative amounts of various additives in the must our fruits can be used to make several different types of wine.

Using traditional country wine recipes the drinks that were made were generally sweet, high alcohol dessert wines, mainly because these have a far greater resistance to attack by micro-organisms; it is the light table wines that are most readily attacked and, due to their lack of body, accentuate the off-flavours of a diseased wine. When wines were only drunk in small quantities, on special occasions, the dessert type was ideal; but today far greater quantities are drunk and more is known about them. Consequently there have been many attempts — with varying degrees of success — to make wines (at home) similar to those that are sold, or to produce country wines still retaining the unique character of the original ingredient, but designed for a specific purpose.

PLANNING YOUR OWN RECIPES

Some ingredients lend themselves to one type of wine rather than another, whilst others such as blackberry and elderberry are ideal for making all types of red wine. With the wide range of ingredients available to the home winemaker the recipes that can be formulated are infinite, and this is the reason why researching through different books it is possible to find several different ways of making a wine from the same ingredient. The recipes included in this book are based on many years experience, and whilst I am sure everyone using them will be delighted with the results, they are by no means the only possible recipes and they indicate only part of the scope of the hobby.

As your knowledge of wines and winemaking increases, you may feel that you wish to adjust recipes to bring out some particular characteristic of a wine or to be completely independent of other people's recipes and formulate your own. Providing you are prepared to do just a little more work and to invest in some cheap, simple to use equipment then this will present no problems.

First you must understand what is meant by the term the balance of the wine, this can only be learnt in part from a book and will be better understood when you have tasted a few bottles of wine — the most enjoyable of all parts of your education.

The balance is the relationship that exists between the main features that make up a wine. These are sweetness, alcohol, acid, tannin, body and, most important, flavour. The general rule is that all six should mutually complement each other, i.e. they should all be high, all be low or all be intermediate. If one of the features predominates then the major, perhaps the only, sensation that you will experience when drinking the wine is that one particular aspect.

Port wine contains unfermented sugars, and although we are aware of the wine being sweet, because all of the other constituents are high it is not the sensation of sweetness that we experience, but that of the drink being right in every respect. At the other end of the scale are the table wines. These are dry but with only 10–12% alcohol, coupled with a light body and low acidity it is a feeling of cleaning the mouth rather than a lack of sweetness that we experience. Between the two extremes lies a whole spectrum of wines, the main types and their composition are summarised in the table (*see* page 19. Once these are known and the methods of controlling them understood, then making any type of wine becomes easy.

We have already considered part of the relationship between sugar and alcohol; and although the maximum amount of alcohol that can be obtained is fixed by the yeast's tolerance, below this figure both the degree of alcohol and the residual sweetness can be controlled.

THE HYDROMETER

It is not possible to state accurately the amount of sugar present in a fruit or in additives such as raisins as these vary with varieties and the seasons. Long hot summers tend to produce relatively high sugar levels, whereas wet, cold years result in high acid levels. This presents no problem if you follow the standard recipes since constituents of wines may be varied by greater limits than result from seasonal variations and still leave the balance virtually unaltered. But if you are going to compound your own recipes it is necessary to know the sugar level already present in the fruit before deciding how much extra should be added. This may be determined by using a hydrometer.

Basically a hydrometer is a hollow glass tube weighted at one end so that it floats upright in a liquid. In liquids that are not very dense the instrument will almost sink, with only the top of the tube not submerged, whereas with a very dense liquid virtually all of the tube floats. The instrument is calibrated by marking the position at the top of the tube in a known low density liquid and the position at the bottom of a known high density liquid. The scale in between is then divided equally to give the calibration. The specific gravity of water is one and should you damage the hydrometer you can always ensure that it is still functioning correctly by checking it against water. Some winemakers refer to the specific gravity not as 1.000 but as zero, this is very misleading as the gravity of table wines is often as low as 0.995 and confusion exists as to how a gravity of less than what they believe to be nought can occur. The gravity above one is due almost entirely to fermentable sugars, but as these are converted to alcohol the density of the liquid may fall below 1.000 as it is now mainly a mixture of water and alcohol and the latter, when pure, has a specific gravity of 0.800.

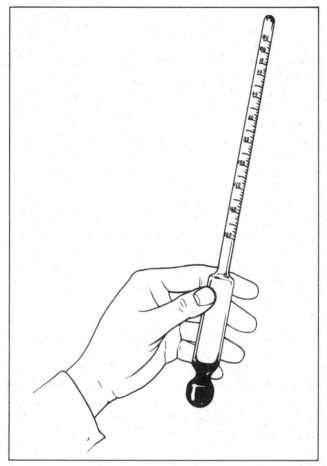

a hydrometer

To use the hydrometer, place the instrument in a hydrometer pot; if this does not come with the instrument, a tall glass or vase will suffice. Give it a gentle turn and read the calibration where the stem comes to rest. You will see that the liquid appears to rise up the stem of the instrument, the correct gravity is obtained by reading the level where the surface of the liquid just meets the stem.

The hydrometer is calibrated at 60°F (16°C), you may ignore the temperature if it deviates by less than two or three degrees. For larger differences, you should add 0.001 for every 3°F (1.5°C) the temperature is above 60°F (16°C). For temperatures below this value a similar amount should be subtracted from the reading.

Two errors can result from using the hydrometer. First, if the wine is still working the carbon dioxide will give extra buoyancy, making the instrument float higher, giving a high result. Second, since some of the materials that will cause the instrument to rise are not fermentable, the reading although accurate may be slightly above the true sugar level. But with wine making we

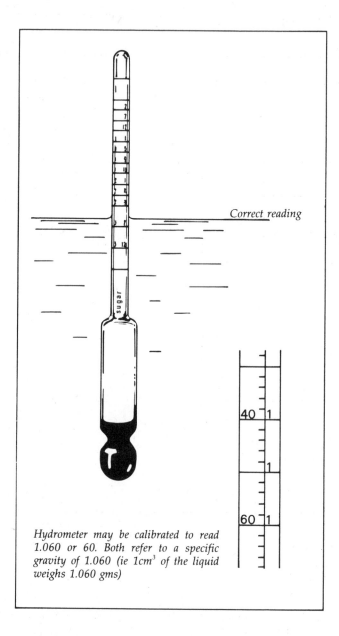

Correct reading

40 1

1

60 1

Hydrometer may be calibrated to read 1.060 or 60. Both refer to a specific gravity of 1.060 (ie 1cm³ of the liquid weighs 1.060 gms)

do not need to be one hundred per cent accurate and remember the instrument used as a basis for levying taxes on beer works on the same principle, so it cannot be far out.

Once you have determined the gravity of the fruit juice and decided what initial gravity you require, then an addition of 5 oz sugar to the gallon (125 gm per 4.5 litres) raises the gravity to 0.010. If your juices have a gravity of 1.040 and you wish to make it up to 1.120 then you will require 1.120–1.040 × 5 × 100 = 40 oz or 2½ lbs.

THE BALANCE OF THE MAIN TYPES

Type of wine	Starting gravity	Finishing gravity	Acidity P P T	Approx. alcohol	Body
White Dry Table	1.080	1.000 or Less	4	12% or Less	Low
White Sweet Table	1.090	1.005 1.010	5	13%	Med
Red Dry Table	1.080	1.000 or Less	4-5	12% or Less	Low
Social	1.100	1.005 1.010	5	13-14%	Med
Dessert Wine	1.120	1.015 1.020	6-8	16%	High
Aperitif (Dry)	1.120	1.000	6	16%	Med
Aperitif (Sweet)	1.120	1.005 1.010	6	16%	Med

It is easier and more accurate to add the sugar, as a syrup, to six pints of liquid and dilute to the gallon.

Obviously the liquid will be less dense when diluted, only 6/8th of its value in the concentrated form, so you allow for this in your calculation.

If you have six pints of a liquid of gravity 1.032 and you wish to make it up to a gallon of density 1.080 then you will require

$$1.080 \ - \frac{1.032 \times 6}{8} \times \frac{5}{0.010} = 28 \text{ oz} = 1 \text{ lb } 12 \text{ oz}$$

STRENGTH OF WINES

Many winemakers like to know how much alcohol is present in their wine, and an approximate figure — many errors are involved as a result of the inefficient conversion during the aerobic fermentation stage — can be obtained by using the hydrometer. Every drop of 0.010 density units corresponds to a potential alcohol of 1.25%, so if the starting gravity was 1.120 and the finishing value was 1.000 then the percentage alcohol is given by

$$1.120 - 1.000 \times 1.25 \times 100 = 16\%$$

A third very important use of the hydrometer is knowing when to stop a wine if you are not fermenting to dryness. If you wish to have the residual sweetness corresponding to a gravity of 1.005, then check the progress of fermentation and when it reaches this value add one Campden tablet and one gram of potassium sorbate which kills the yeast. When high alcohol concentration above 14% is sought it is better to allow fermentation to proceed to dryness and sweeten the wine rather than initially to increase the gravity above 1.120. Although the finished gravity of a dessert wine should be 1.015–1.020 this figure can only be reached by the addition of sugar after fermentation is complete.

ACID TESTING

Providing there is sufficient acid present in the must, as will always be the case if the standard recipes are followed, a smooth fermentation will result. But where non standard recipes are being used it is advisable to check the acid levels with an acid testing kit. These work on the basis of measuring from a dropper the amount of a substance that neutralises the acid. When the neutralisation is complete, an indicator changes colour. You simply read off the volume of neutralising agent required to react with a certain amount of the must and multiply by a factor given in the instructions.

Some people do experience a degree of difficulty seeing the colour change in red wines, but if you look carefully you will see a darkening of colour with the liquid going either a deep shade of purple or brown, depending on the other colouring material present. If you have access to fluorescent lighting then it is far easier to see the colour change in red wines.

Since these kits are always sold with instructions and there may be variations from one kit to another, I will give no further details other than to say that they are cheap, accurate and easy to use.

Acid levels obtained by this method are calculated in parts per thousand (p.p.t.). Some authorities recommend using the pH scale. Due to difficulties in determining pH, papers are not accurate enough for most purposes, electronic meters are too expensive and the calculations to adjust pH are beyond all but qualified chemists, I would recommend that the amateur forgets the concept of pH entirely.

Once you have determined the acid level, raising it presents no problems.

One level 5 ml teaspoonful of citric acid raises the acid level of one gallon of wine by 2 p.p.t. If smaller amounts are required, such as 0.5 p.p.t., simply dissolve in water and divide the thoroughly stirred solution by four.

Far more of a problem is too much acid. The factor which decides how much fruit to use is the amount of acid it will provide in a gallon of must. Recipes stipulate a specific amount of fruit. If you use extra fruit, you will not make a better wine, but an inferior wine due to the excess of acid present. Should you feel that the fruit has produced a must too high in acid, add sufficient extra fruit to provide enough juice to make two gallons of wine.

There are on the market various preparations that will lower the acid level of a must. Keep your wine making as simple as possible. The over use of chemicals, as well as making wine making more complicated, often takes something away from the quality of the finished wine. Particularly avoid the use of powdered chalk as wines treated in this way are nearly always impossible to clear; this compound is often recommended for use with rhubarb. Rhubarb makes a superb wine, but unless carefully treated is over acid, for this reason it is inadvisable to deviate from the recipe given. Rhubarb wine is excellent for blending with other wines, so if you wish to incorporate its unique characteristics, add it to another clear wine after it has cleared.

TANNIN

Acidity of a wine is often confused with excess of tannin, both of which are harsh to the taste, but without them a wine is dull and uninteresting. Both are needed in the right amounts. Acid is detected at the back of the mouth and tannin on the gums and the inside of the cheeks. There is no test that can be performed in the kitchen for tannin, but if you think that the level is too low, extra can be added to the wine after it has cleared. If the tannin is too high, then this will only disappear with maturation. High tannin is probably the most important single reason why red wines, both commercial and country, need excessively long maturation periods. The role of tannin in winemaking is still not fully understood, but it appears to be necessary to help the clearing process, and should always be present to some extent at the commencement of fermentation. It is not possible to generalise on tannin as virtually every ingredient has to be treated differently to ensure the correct amount is present. Where there is insufficient tannin this can be added to the must in one of three ways.

The simplest and cheapest is to add a cup of cold tea, but the disadvantage with this method is that the amount of tannin will differ according to the type of teas used and the period of time it was mashed for. If you want to be sure of adding a standard amount use grape tannin solution, which can now be bought in most homebrew centres, dispensed from a dropper. You can make several gallons from one bottle and it works out very cheap. Where either raisins or sultanas are included in the recipe the alcohol formed during the early stages of fermentation will extract sufficient tannin from the skins of one pound of the fruit for most wines. This is probably the most common method of providing tannin.

BODY

By far the most expensive aspect of home winemaking is providing sufficient body. Wines lacking body are thin to the taste and have a watery texture, whereas wines with body tend to have weight when held in the mouth. Body results from the presence in the wine of unfermentable compounds, the most important of which is glycerine. Few of our natural fruits which are otherwise well suited to winemaking contain these compounds in sufficient quantities and we must add other fruits to give this characteristic. Without a doubt, sultanas are the most useful, providing body, sugar and a certain amount of acid. These are superior to raisins, whose strong flavour can predominate in a delicate wine, although with some ingredients the situation may be reversed in that they provide some of the body, but little flavour. In such cases strong flavoured raisins are required to provide the wine with the necessary taste. If you use either sultanas or raisins it is important that the extraction is efficient. This can only be achieved if the fruit is thoroughly broken up, otherwise the mixture of water and newly formed alcohol will only dissolve compounds from the skin of the fruit, and the sugars and body-giving ingredients will be thrown away after straining. By far the most efficient way of preparing sultanas is to place them in a liquidiser with an equal volume of water for about five seconds. If the mixture does not form a puree, then the process may be repeated. If you are using raisins then ensure that it is the seedless variety, otherwise the seeds will break and release oils that will give the wine a bitter taste.

If you do not possess a liquidiser then raisins and sultanas may be chopped or minced, the latter method is preferred as it makes considerably less work.

One of the biggest advantages of using sultanas or raisins is that as well as providing body, and certain other compounds, it gives the wine vinosity or wine-like character and bouquet. You can provide this with grape juice concentrate and although half a can of concentrate can be used instead of one pound of sultanas it is almost twice as expensive. If you use half a can of concentrate, you may keep the remainder in a sealed container in the refrigerator. But to avoid the dangers of infection it is better to make another batch of wine at the same time.

The cheapest of all ingredients for providing body is overripe bananas. Do not buy better quality fruit since the body-giving chemicals have only fully developed when they are passed their best. These can often be purchased very cheaply from a greengrocer, and providing they are peeled and any decayed fruit discarded they are excellent. It is only the water soluble material in the banana that is required, and this is obtained by boiling the fruit for about twenty minutes in an equal volume of water. Always strain and discard the pulp, never ferment in the presence of bananas and do not use the skins, otherwise the wine will have a strong banana flavour that will never disappear. If you have access to a cheap supply of fresh figs, these may be used for providing the wine with body. Use two pounds (1 kg) of figs, cut them in half and incorporate them in the must, in place of the sultanas. Do not use both sultanas and figs, unless stipulated in the recipe.

Figs are slightly inferior to sultanas, so do not be tempted to use dried figs that are usually more expensive than sultanas.

Crushed wheat was used for many years as a cheap substitute for sultanas; although the wines usually lack vinosity, this ingredient is a very useful alternative. To use wheat, simply replace the sultanas with an equal quantity of the cereal and add, if available, amylase to prevent starch haze formation. Again, unless specified in the recipe, do not use both wheat and sultanas.

Malt has been recommended for giving body to a wine, but this ingredient should be avoided, because if it is used in sufficient quantities to improve the texture its overpowering flavour comes through and spoils the wine.

FLAVOUR AND BOUQUET

Flavour and bouquet are perhaps the two most important factors in a wine. It is difficult to predict the flavour of a wine, because unless it is drunk whilst quite young, it will not necessarily have the characteristic flavour of the fruits from which it was made. Again the fundamental rules of balance apply: with full bodied dessert wines both flavour and bouquet should be well developed, but with a table wine the flavour should be subtle, as should the bouquet. The bouquet of a table wine should be like a lady's perfume, only those entitled to enjoy it should know of its existence.

It is only with experience that you will realise how much fruit or how many flowerheads to use to get the right flavour and balance. The amount of a fruit such as peaches, delicious in small amounts but overpowering when used in excess, that we employ are governed not by the amount of acid present but by the flavour!

The choice of the correct recipe, the selection of the fruit, fully ripe but with all decayed pieces removed, and the manner in which it is treated are the most important factors in influencing the quality of the finished wine. For whilst it is possible to improve the wine by blending, and other various treatments, you will never make really great wines unless you take care to compound a balanced must or use a tried and tested recipe.

T·H·E· T·E·C·H·N·I·Q·U·E·S· O·F·
W·I·N·E·M·A·K·I·N·G

With increased interest in winemaking several different methods of making the wine have evolved. No one method is applicable to all wines, because of the variety of ingredients used.

EXTRACTION AND STERILISATION OF THE MUST

Of prime importance is an efficient method of extracting the juices and soluble material from the fruit. Since no fruit, with the exception of the grape, provides all the liquid required, the bulk of the water must be provided by the vintner. It is at the start, when the water is added, that any wild yeast or other micro organisms present must be killed, because precautions taken throughout fermentation are to prevent infection, not to cure any disorders that are already present in the wine. If the fruit is not sterilised at the initial stage, the wine will probably be irreversibly ruined.

THE HOT METHOD

There are two methods of extraction and sterilising musts, both have advantages and disadvantages, but on balance the best method is to cover the fruit with boiling water. Theoretically some germs might survive the treatment, but I have never had an infected must as a result of making wines by this method and it involves a far higher temperature than pasteurisation, which is considered a sufficient treatment for most food stuffs. The solubility of most materials increases with rise in temperature and boiling water increases the efficiency of extraction over the cold water method. It is argued that the higher temperature either destroys or evaporates some of the more delicate fragrances that produce flavour and bouquet in a wine, but this is seldom the case. With some fruit, boiling water does destroy the enzymes which stop the formation of pectin, the gelatinous substance that causes jams to set. Pectin causes hazes, which are often almost impossible to remove even from the finished wine, and for this reason pectic enzyme should be added to the must together with the yeast. As the pectic enzyme is chemically similar to that naturally present in the fruit; never add it before the must has cooled otherwise it will also be destroyed. The addition of pectic enzyme is a precautionary step and has no effect on the taste of the finished wine; although it is included in most of the recipes, if you wish to make wines without 'chemical treatments' it may be omitted, but it must be remembered that there is always a chance of the haze forming. Where you elect not to use pectic enzyme do not cut or mince either raisin or sultanas, as these often appear to be the cause of the haze. Always add pectic enzyme to any liquid that has been obtained by steam extraction. Should you omit the enzyme, and a haze does develop, sometimes — depending upon the type of wine —

it is possible to add it after fermentation is complete. This is not as reliable however as adding the enzyme at the start of fermentation, as it is destroyed by alcohol and treatment is only usually effective at this stage with the weaker table wines.

With the exception of bananas and a few others, fruit should never be boiled and simmered. For although it is an efficient method of both extraction and sterilisation, so much pectin is released that subsequent enzyme treatment will not stop permanent haze formation. Too much flavouring material is lost and unless you are very careful sugars naturally present in the fruit will caramelise, giving the finished wine a maderised taste, which will detract from the flavour in all but the fullest dessert wines.

Roots such as parsnips, however, need boiling for efficient extraction. Like fruits, roots form haze due in this instance to starch. Starch haze can be treated even after boiling with the enzyme amylase and this should be added in the same way as pectic enzyme. Again if you wish to minimise the chemical treatment it may be omitted.

THE COLD METHOD

The alternative method of preparing musts is by soaking the fruit in cold water. By using this method there is no need to add enzymes and there is no danger of damaging the delicate chemical structure of the fragrances. But the problems come with sterilisation, which is brought about by the addition of either one Campden tablet or 5 ml of a ten per cent solution of sodium metabisulphite. Both of these release sulphur dioxide, which kills the micro organisms and during the next twenty four hours is converted to a harmless chemical. After this period the yeast must be immediately added. This is a variation on the method widely used in the commercial production of wines, but the amateur finds that sterilisation is not always effective and residual sulphur dioxide occasionally arrests the yeast's development. Since either problem can lead to the loss of the wine, it is not a good general method.

The role of sulphur dioxide in commercial wine production is not understood by many country winemakers. Not only does it sterilise musts, but it also behaves as a reducing agent, stopping grape juice oxidising to a brown colour. For this reason, if you are making wine from your own grapes or apples — both of which oxidise readily — and you want a white rather than a golden wine, then the sulphur dioxide treatment must be used.

CLARIFICATION

Good wines can be made with very little effort — it is surprising how little work is required if you follow the few basic rules — but if you wish to make really great country wines then meticulous attention to detail is necessary. Nowhere is this more obvious than with clarification, which is often thought of as a corrective measure at the completion of the winemaking process. If steps are taken at the commencement of winemaking to obviate hazes then problems do not arise that require expensive filters, or the addition of chemicals that always seem to change, albeit slightly, the taste of the wine. The best clearing agent is Bentonite, which should be added, not as is the usual practice, when fermentation is complete, but at the same time as the yeast. Bentonite is a porous sand-like material, that clears the wine by trapping minute particles in its microscopic sieve-like orifices. If it is added prior to fermentation then the carbon dioxide liberated will agitate the grains giving the effect of several minute filters moving up and down during the early stages of winemaking. When fermentation ceases it will come to rest with other sediments at the bottom of the demijohn and is separated off by racking. The addition of Bentonite at this stage is optional but if you decide to use it, the day before it is required place an ounce in a sterilised container, cover with water and leave covered for twenty four hours. This produces a thick paste which is then added to the wine. The Bentonite may be added at any time during the early fermentation stage, some winemakers preferring to wait until the must has been transferred to the demijohn.

STARTING THE WINE

When the juice has been extracted and the yeast and enzymes added, check that after forty eight hours (twenty four if using a yeast starter bottle) the fermentation has started working, initially this will only be seen as a slight effervescence. If after two days there is no sign of activity then add a fresh supply of yeast. Once fermentation has started the vigorous head will rapidly form. Stir every day during this time; if the fermentation is conducted in the presence of solid fruit as opposed to liquid, break as much of it as possible against the side of the bucket when the vigorous head has subsided. If there is no solid material, other than the slight deposit that always forms at the start of the fermentation, transfer straight to the demijohn. Where fruit is present strain through muslin into a second bucket before placing in a demijohn. It is impossible to say exactly how much liquid you will possess at this stage, because the amount present in various fruit varies so much from season to season, but you will need, in most instances, to top up the container to the neck with tap water. Do not bother to boil the water, for although this has been suggested to ensure complete sterility, surely the water that we drink untreated ourselves is good enough for winemaking.

When fitting an air lock of the type that requires water, and most of them do, ensure that there is sufficient water present. Again tap water will suffice, the practice of using a solution of metabisulphite is pointless on two counts. Firstly it is highly unlikely that the micro organisms that attack wine can survive and pass through the water which contains none of its necessary nutrients, and secondly the sulphur dioxide which the chemical releases will be dispersed in the atmosphere after twenty four hours. What must be realised though is that the water will, at the higher temperature of the fermentation cabinet, rapidly evaporate and the airlocks should be inspected at regular intervals to ensure that they have not dried out. Failure to do this may result in a spoilt wine as a dry airlock offers no protection at all.

During fermentation the wine benefits greatly from being shaken every day, this dispels the carbon dioxide and encourages the newly formed alcohol to leave the immediate vicinity of the yeast. But do not worry if you do not have the time to do this as it is perhaps the least important of operations. I know one winemaker who actually talks to his fermenting wine; so be warned and do not drink too much of it!

RACKING

The wine needs no further attention until it has been made for two months, sooner if a quarter inch (0.5 cm) of sediment has formed at the bottom of the vessel. At this stage the debris of dead yeast and fruit cells should be separated from the liquid, which will probably still not be clear. This is done by a process known as racking. For this you will require a racking tube, again the simpler the better, consisting of a U tube and length of plastic as described under equipment. Place the demijohn of wine on the kitchen work bench with the minimum amount of agitation, and a previously sterilised demijohn on the floor. Insert the U tube so that its bottom is touching the bottom of the demijohn. The short upward part of the racking tube will ensure that none of the sediment is carried over with the wine. Syphon the liquid by sucking through the tube and placing your finger over the end of the tube which should then be inserted into the empty demijohn. Discard the sediment that remains in the first jar and wash immediately, as dried yeast sediments are almost impossible to remove.

The wine will not fill the second container and if you have added all the sugar specified in the recipe you will need to add tap water to make up to the original volume. Do not worry about the dilution effect because a good recipe will have allowed for this. If the recipe calls for extra sugar then this should be added at this stage dissolved in the minimum amount of water.

The experienced winemaker will learn a lot from his wine at the racking stage from the small quantity that he swallows; you will soon acquire the experience to assess the quality from just a sip.

When you begin winemaking you might like to pour yourself half a glass to assess the progress of the wine. It may even have finished working if it is a light dry table wine, in which case you will not detect any sweetness, which is noticeable immediately the wine enters the mouth. Nor if you "chew" the wine will you detect the tingling sensation that tells you carbon dioxide is escaping as a result of continuing fermentation. For a more objective view of how fermentation is progressing you can check the gravity with a hydrometer, and provided that sterilised equipment is used the sample can afterwards be returned safely to the bulk. Any wine still working, and most will be at this stage, should be returned to the fermentation cabinet.

Do not rack again until the wine has stopped working, unless you see a sediment of at least quarter of an inch (0.5 cm). This will be noticed when bubbles cease to escape from the airlock. As before this may be checked by the hydrometer. The wine should now be clear.

After the final racking, which should be conducted in the same manner as the first, the wine may again be topped up with tap water if it is going to be

1. Place demijohn of wine on kitchen surface with clean, sterilised demijohn below.

2. Put end of racking tube with 'U' bend into the wine taking care not to disturb the lees.

3. Suck the tube until the liquid enters the mouth.

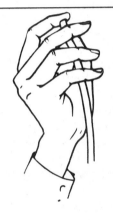

Place finger over the end of the tube and insert into the lower, empty demijohn.

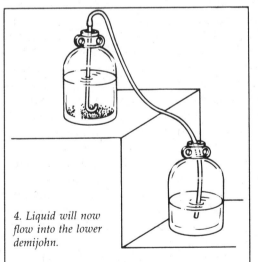

4. Liquid will now flow into the lower demijohn.

5. Top up with tap water and fit air lock or cork.

stored in bulk, or be bottled. But immediately prior to this the wine can be stabilised with 1 crushed Campden tablet and 1 gram potassium sorbate per gallon (do not worry about the weight, containers are supplied with easy measures.) In the past only Campden tablets were added, but these do not completely stop refermentations, the potassium sorbate is far more effective. If you add potassium sorbate without the Campden tablet that undergoes reaction with it, the wine develops a geranium-like bouquet and flavour that makes it undrinkable. With white wines it is essential to add a Campden tablet to stop browning if you want a well coloured wine. Campden tablets should be crushed before use, this is best done by grinding a tablet between two teaspoons, otherwise they will not dissolve and liberate sufficient sulphur dioxide to kill the bacteria. They are only effective if the total available sterilant is released together. Moreover a Campden tablet dissolving over a period of several weeks may leave an objectionable taste and render the wine undrinkable for months. Some winemakers never use Campden tablets and still produce excellent wines. Wines which are made from three or more pounds of sugar per gallon are unlikely to support any wine spoilage organism as the alcohol level will be too high. Unless you are concerned about the colour or wish to make low alcohol table wine, omit the addition of Campden tablets.

We have discussed the general factors and their relative importance in winemaking, but special types of wine require special treatments.

TABLE WINES

These being low in alcohol ferment out more rapidly and may well be ready for drinking after the first racking, at which stage they may be bottled.

SOCIAL WINES

These include wines designed to be drunk without a meal and usually they contain a certain amount of residual sweetness. Since their alcohol level should not be as high as the maximum that the yeast will tolerate, otherwise you will be too restricted in the amount that you can drink, it is best to ferment to dryness and sweeten the wine after fermentation has ceased. Where a wine is to be sweetened, it should be stabilised by the addition of both a Campden tablet and potassium sorbate. It is preferable to do this in the bottle to ensure that the sugar marries with the wine. Most social wines are drunk at a gravity of 1.005–1.010. Addition of one ounce (25 gm) of sugar per bottle raises the gravity by approximately 0.012.

DESSERT WINES

These are the fullest of all wines, and should have the highest possible alcohol. This can only be achieved by 'feeding the wine'. If too much sugar i.e. more than three pounds (1.5 kg) per gallon are used the fermentation will cease prematurely due to the combined effects of the alcohol and sugar. Maximum conversion can only be achieved if the sugar is added in a solution of a quarter of a pound (110 gm) dissolved in an eighth of a pint (65 ml) of water each time the gravity of the wine drops to 1.000. When fermentation finally ceases the gravity should be increased to 1.015–1.020. These wines require the largest maturation period, but do appear to keep indefinitely. I had a twenty five year old elderberry that was superb.

Alternatively to obtain slightly lower concentrations of alcohol, though still higher than those achieved by standard procedure, add extra sugar either when the wine is transferred to the demijohn, when some of the initial sugar will have fermented, or after the first racking. Where this is necessary, details are given in the recipes.

ROSÉ WINES

Some ingredients, such as raspberries, do tend to give a rose coloured wine but the best way to make this type is to prepare a light white table wine such as gooseberry (for recipe see February) then add blackcurrant fruit juice. The small quantities required to colour the wine will not adversely affect the taste. Alternatively you may use cochineal for colouring purposes.

SPARKLING WINES

There can be few people who do not enjoy a really good sparkling wine and although we can never hope to produce a Vintage Champagne, with a little care and attention it is possible to make a sparkling wine to celebrate those special occasions, or for just sitting back and enjoying.

The sparkle is produced by allowing the wine to finish its fermentation in the bottle and it is the naturally manufactured carbon dioxide that is responsible for the effervescence. Great care must be taken to ensure that the bottles do not burst and the wine should only be stored in champagne bottles weighing about 900 gms. Some other bottles could be used, but not all commercial sparkling wines are made by secondary fermentation in the bottle and those which are artificially carbonated can be controlled so critically that the manufacturers are able to use a cheaper bottle. Such bottles cannot be guaranteed to withstand the high pressures that may develop in home made sparkling wines.

Whilst any dry table wine recipe is suitable for conversion into a sparkling wine, the best results are usually obtained from gooseberry wine as given in the February recipe or the rhubarb champagne given in the May recipes. Special techniques and meticulous attention to detail are necessary to make this type of wine.

It is the only type of wine where it is necessary to use a specialised yeast. Champagne yeast forms as a hard crust at the bottom of the bottle and is capable of withstanding far more agitation than other yeasts, without breaking up. This is very important when the wine is being poured because you want the yeast sediment to remain in the bottle, not in the glass.

To make sparkling wines the progress of fermentation must be followed carefully with the hydrometer and when the gravity has dropped to exactly

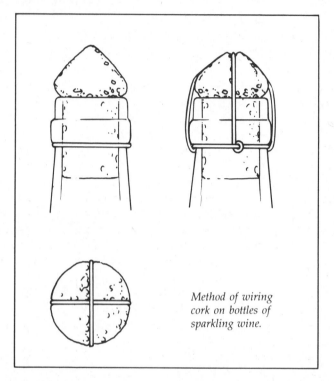

Method of wiring cork on bottles of sparkling wine.

1.000 the wine should be racked off. It is then bottled, without the addition of Campden tablets or other treatment, in the champagne bottles. Do not add extra sugar at this stage. It is necessary to wire the corks down to stop them blowing as a result of the pressure generated. This is done by fixing a collar of packing case type wire around the neck of the bottle. A second piece of wire is hooked under the collar and tightened with pliers and then brought over the top of the cork. It is then hooked under the opposite side of the collar and tightened. The process is repeated with a second piece of wire, so that a cross is formed at the top of the cork.

The bottles should then be placed in the fermentation cabinet for a month, after which time they will be ready for drinking. When serving sparkling wines the greatest care should be taken as very high pressures are involved. Always stand the wine in the refrigerator two hours before serving as sparkling wines are only at their best when chilled. Wrap the bottle in a tea towel and undo the wire with pliers, making sure that you do not agitate the bottle before opening.

An alternative method of making sparkling wines, is to allow the wine to ferment out completely, the gravity may be well below 1.000, and then to add half a teaspoonful of sugar per bottle. Return to the fermentation cabinet and finish in the same manner as above.

Making sparkling wines requires a little more effort than some wines, but when you have tasted your first glass you will realise that it was worth it.

SHERRY TYPE WINES

Sherry is different from every other type of wine in that it is deliberately oxidised. It is the high alcohol and flavouring that allows sherry to be treated in this way. Parsnips and prunes are probably the best ingredient for dry sherry making and full instructions are given in the recipes. Oxidation should be controlled and seldom requires longer than a fortnight to a month, but the only way to ensure that you have the correct flavour is to sample the wine periodically and as soon as you think that the flavour is right stop the oxidation. There are many different ways of bringing about this oxidation. The best way is to wait until fermentation is complete as it is the alcohol you wish to oxidise. At this stage divide the liquid equally in two demijohns, both fitted with an air lock. When your palate tells you that oxidation is complete recombine both liquids in one demijohn for storage, alternatively you may bottle the wine. Commercial sherries are fortified with brandy, and you may do this — try the addition of two fluid ounces (50 ml) to the bottle.

Commercially there are several different types of sherry but the amateur must restrict himself to two, sweet and dry. Sweet sherry is best made from prunes (see March) and treated in the same way as dry sherry described above, but should be sweetened by the addition of glycerine and a non fermentable sweetener such as lactose. Do not sweeten with sugar as it may referment.

Under no circumstances should Campden tablets be used with a sherry type wine as the sulphur dioxide released reacts with the oxidation products, destroying the unique flavours.

Either sweet or dry sherries can be improved by the addition of sherry type essences, these are best added to taste immediately prior to bottling.

It is possible to make very good imitation sherries, but the cost of additives such as brandy and essence do tend to make it the most expensive of all wines, nevertheless it is still far cheaper than anything that can be bought in the shops.

THREE WEEK WINES

During recent years, a number of winemaking kits have appeared on the market which allow you to make wine that is ready for drinking in about a month. These make very acceptable table wines.

It is possible to make these from a wide variety of readily available fruits and juices which is far cheaper than using kits. However, making these wines involves special techniques and recipes, different from those used in general winemaking, and the methods are discussed in *Winemaking from Kits* (Prism Press).

M·A·K·I·N·G T·H·E W·I·N·E

STERILISING EQUIPMENT

When making wine it is essential to ensure that all equipment is absolutely sterile. Not only must the fruit for winemaking be absolutely free from airborne yeast and bacteria, so must all equipment used. Even if apparatus appears to be clean it may still harbour microscopic spores which will thrive under the same conditions as those so carefully created for the yeast, AN INFECTED PIECE OF EQUIPMENT AT ANY STAGE CAN SPOIL YOUR WINE.

Cloths used for straining are best boiled in water, stainless steel colanders may also be made sterile by standing in a saucepan in which the cloths are boiled. No type of metal other than stainless steel should be allowed to come into contact with the wine. All plastic and glass equipment can be sterilised by placing in a bucket, one designed for using in winemaking is ideal, with an ounce (25 gm) of sodium metabisulphite solution and half a teaspoonful of citric acid added to a pint (0.5 litre) of cold water, leave standing for twenty four hours. The equipment should be washed thoroughly and it is then ready for use. Care should be taken not to inhale the fumes from the sterilising mixture which can damage the lungs.

A quicker method of sterilising glass and plastic is by using domestic bleach, but as this is such a strong poison the greatest care must be taken not to inhale the fumes and to ensure that the equipment is thoroughly washed after use. Six or seven washings with cold water are necessary to ensure that the items sterilised in this way are safe to use. Apart from the disadvantage, it is the cheapest, quickest and most efficient sterilising agent available to the home winemaker. Place about one fluid ounce (25 ml) — do not try to measure the volume, guess it — and a pint (0.5 litre) of water in the fermenting bucket together with the equipment, fit the lid and then leave for half an hour. The equipment is ready for use after thorough washing. There are now available cleaning and sterilising powders specially developed for home wine and beer making. These are completely effective and have the advantage that they will clean as well as sterilise equipment. These are more expensive than bleach. When all equipment is sterile you are ready to make the wine.

STAGE 1 (OPTIONAL SEE BELOW)

Prepare a yeast starter by placing 3oz (75 gm) of sugar, tip of a teaspoonful of citric acid, half a teaspoonful of dried yeast and half a pint (250 ml) of water in a sterilised milk bottle. Cover with a plastic film and place in the fermentation cabinet.

STAGE 2

Prepare the must according to the instructions given in the recipe. When the temperature has dropped to 70°F (21°C) or that nearest to the conditions at

1. Gather together: fermenting bucket, sterilising solution, fruit, yeast, enzymes, raisins, etc.

2. Remove any decayed pieces of fruit and wash well under running water.

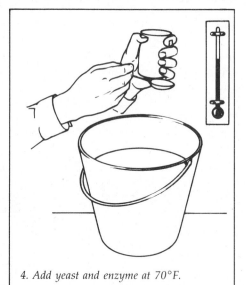

3. Place the fruit in a sterilised bucket with boiling water, cover the fementation bucket with an air-tight lid.

4. Add yeast and enzyme at 70°F.

5. Stir the wine daily until the vigorous fermentation ceases.

6. Sieve through a colander lined with muslin: alternatively use a winemaking sieve.

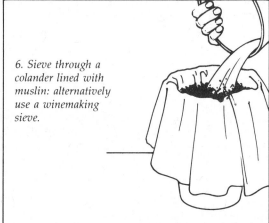

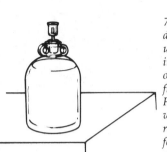

7. Place a demijohn, top up to within an inch (2.54 cm) of the top and fit an air lock. Fill air lock with water and return to fermentation cabinet.

8. When there is ¼'' (0.5 cm) of sediment, rack.

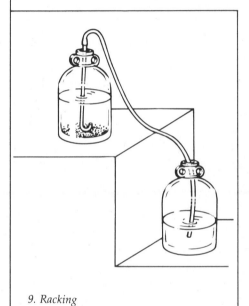

9. Racking

10. After racking top up with tap water, refit air lock and return to fermentation cabinet until bubbles cease to escape from the air lock.

Rerack the wine and add one crushed campden tablet and one gram of potassium sorbate.

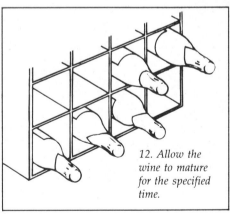

12. Allow the wine to mature for the specified time.

11. Bottle, cork, label and cap.

13. Serve!!

which you intend conducting the fermentation, add the yeast from the starter bottle, any recommended enzymes and half a teaspoonful of yeast nutrient.

Take one tablespoonful of Bentonite, mix with a small quantity of water. Leave to stand for 24 hours before adding the paste to the must (optional).

If you did not prepare a yeast starter, and this is only essential where specified in the recipe, twenty four hours before commencing your brew, half a teaspoonful of dried yeast must be added at this stage.

STAGE 3

Stir the must daily, taking care to break up any solid fruit that may be present. Watch for the development and subsidence of the voluminous head. Check that the total volume is one gallon, or 4.5 litres if using metric units. It is not always possible to predict the volume accurately as fruits, even of the same variety, can differ quite considerably in the volume of juice which they yield. Where a bucket is used where the gallon level is not denoted, measure one gallon of water (4.5 litres) into it prior to use and mark the position on the side of the container.

STAGE 4

When the initial head has subsided, usually after four to ten days according to the recipe and temperature, strain the juice through muslin into the demijohn. Top up with water to the neck of the demijohn and fit an airlock. Occasionally if you are using very juicy fruit you may have more than a gallon (4.5 litres) of liquid at this stage. If this should happen it is best to discard the excess, for although it might seem wasteful, odd half pints of liquid almost invariably become infected and produce a sour wine.

STAGE 5

Gently agitate the demijohns every other day and check to ensure that the air lock has not dried out.

STAGE 6

After two months, or sooner if the wine has more than an half inch (1 cm) of sediment, rack the wine by syphoning into another demijohn. Top up with water, refit airlock and return to the fermentation cabinet.

STAGE 7

If no further heavy sediment forms leave the wine to clear, rerack. Add 1 Campden tablet and 1 gram of potassium sorbate, should you decide to use the chemical treatment, which is only essential if specified in the recipe. If a second heavy sediment occurs stage 6 should be repeated.

The month after the treatment with Campden tablet (if used) it is safe to drink the wine. If no chemical treatment has been applied the wine may be drunk as soon as it is clear. In either case it may not be fully matured at this stage.

THE NO CHEMICAL METHOD OF WINEMAKING

Making wines by the above method will be virtually trouble free and you can almost guarantee a good wine every time. However there are people who prefer to make wines by a no chemical method, arguing that 'My grandmother never messed about with fancy methods and made good wines all her life'. Up to a point this is true. Old recipes advocated the use of ingredients that today would be too expensive; that made wines so full that they possessed inborn protection. Today we have not got access to virtually limitless fruit and cheap raisins.

Even more important, with our increasing knowledge of commercial wines we are demanding far better wines than it was thought possible to make a decade ago. We now prefer drier wines and are demanding the same degree of clarity, the old wines were seldom really clear — as found in those we buy. But above all our palates are far more discerning.

Nevertheless there is a move away from foods contaminated by chemicals. It is possible to make excellent wines without the use of manufactured chemicals, which although readily available in many countries, may not be easy to obtain in some areas. Do not let a lack of chemicals or a desire not to use them deter you from winemaking. The recipes given in this book can all be made without the addition of enzymes, although these are naturally occurring, nutrients and Campden tablets. Make the wine in exactly the manner described but omit all manufactured 'chemicals'. Sterilise fruit and utensils with boiling water.

The natural method will generally give you good wines but you must be prepared to wait a little longer, accept a lower standard of clarity and lower alcohol content. If you are careful the wine should not be infected, but under no circumstances attempt to use the so called no yeast method. This relies on the wild yeast naturally present on fruit and failure is the rule rather than the exception with this method.

With experience you may well evolve your own method somewhere between the chemical and natural way of winemaking. There are several good ways of making wine and provided that the method does not break any of the 'golden rules' it will result in many gallons of excellent wine.

W·I·N·E·M·A·K·I·N·G
M·O·N·T·H B·Y M·O·N·T·H

Throughout the text the recipes are quoted in both Imperial (British) and metric units.

The U.S. gallon and pint are slightly smaller than their Imperial equivalents. To avoid confusion, I have quoted recipes as an average of both the British and U.S. units so that the wines may be made in either country without adjusting the weight of the ingredients used.

The quality of the wine will in no way be affected by this approximation as both seasonal variations and the effect of using different varieties of fruits will have far greater influence. Moreover quantities are by no means as critical as is often thought, and for this reason a variation of a quarter to a half a pound (125–250 gm) of the major ingredient will not affect the balance of a gallon (4.5 litres) of wine.

The conversion to metric units is calculated relative to Imperial units.

Where teaspoon (tsp), tablespoon (tbs) and dessertspoons are quoted these refer to the level spoonful.

In the recipes for flower and leaf wines the volume of flowers and leaves quoted, after all twig and green material has been removed, should be measured out by placing in a suitable capacity container without pressing down.

JANUARY

Although root wines may be made at any time between November and March, by January the frost will probably have acted on them, but they will not have begun to shoot. Consequently they are at their best for winemaking. Roots do not provide sufficient body for the wine and it is necessary to include raisins in the recipes. These wines are usually slow maturing and are not at their best until at least a year old.

PARSNIP WINE

Parnsip has a distinctive but not strong flavour, consequently the alcohol comes through in the taste of the finished wine. It is often described as a strong wine but it seldom contains more alcohol than a fruit wine.

4 lb (1.75 kg) parsnips
1 lb (0.5 kg) raisins
2 lb (1 kg) sugar
2 tsp citric acid
pectic enzyme/starch enzyme
yeast

Boil the parsnips in four pints (2 litres) of water until they are soft enough to break with a fork. Strain the liquid into a bucket and discard the parsnips, which may be used for normal culinary purposes. Mince or chop the raisins and add together with the sugar dissolved in two pints (1 litre) of water and the citric acid. At 70°F (21°C) add the yeast, pectic and starch enzymes. Stir the liquid daily until the vigorous head subsides, usually after a week; then strain and place in a demijohn, adding extra water to make up to one gallon (4.5 litres). Fit an air lock and leave until fermentation is complete.
    Three variations of the basic method are possible. For those who prefer

an oxidised sherry type wine after clearing divide the wine into two parts and transfer into two one gallon jars, so that they are both only half full. Cork and leave for a fortnight, but no longer, in a cool place; then recombine.

If you prefer a sweeter wine add an extra half pound (250 gm) of sugar dissolved in the minimum quantity of hot water after the initial racking and return to the fermentation cabinet.

In the old country wine method it was usual to add ½ an ounce (15 gm) of ginger with the raisins. This addition may be made to either the sweet or dry wine.

CARROT WINE

This is based on an old country recipe for carrot whisky. Any comparison with Scotch owes more to the drinker's lack of knowledge of that drink than to the flavour of the carrots. Nevertheless it is a very good country wine in its own right. Old rather than young carrots tend to give the best results.

3 lb (1.5 kg) carrots
1 lb (0.5 kg) wheat
3 lb (1.5 kg) sugar
½ lb (250 gm) raisins
2 tsp citric acid
pectic enzyme/starch enzyme
yeast

Place the carrots in a saucepan with four pints (2 litres) of water and boil until soft. Strain the liquid and transfer to a bucket. The carrots may be used for culinary purposes.

Buy only wheat of a grade fit for human consumption. Wheat on sale in certain pet shops does not always meet this specification. Put the wheat in a cloth bag and crush with a rolling pin or similar heavy implement.

Add the crushed wheat, minced raisins and the sugar dissolved in two pints (1 litre) of water to the carrot juice. Make the total volume up to one gallon (4.5 litres) with tap water, then add the pectic and starch enzymes together with the yeast and citric acid.

This wine often leaves a heavy sediment and should be racked off as soon as this is about ½ inch (1 cm) thick. Leave until clear before racking again.

This will give a medium dry wine, do not add extra sugar as this wine does not lend itself to sweetening.

Variations
You may replace the wheat with an extra half pound (250 gm) of raisins, in which case the starch enzyme should be omitted.

Addition of ginger tends to mask the unique flavour and should not be included.

Delicately flavoured sultanas are lost against the background of the carrots and should not be used.

Never attempt to drink a carrot wine until it is at least one year old.

POTATO WINE

This is another of the traditional country wines. It is a very full and sweet dessert wine that certainly benefits from keeping.

4 lb (2 kg) potatoes
1 lb (0.5 kg) raisins
2½ lb (1.25 kg) white sugar
½ lb (250 gm) demerara sugar
2 oranges
1 lemon
pectic enzyme/starch enzyme
yeast

Peel the potatoes and chop into small pieces, mince the raisins and place together in a bucket. Cover with four pints (2 litres) of boiling water. Dissolve the sugar in two pints of water and add. It is only the juice of the oranges and lemon that is required and any method of juicing may be used. Alternatively peel the fruit and remove all the pieces of white pith — which will give the wine a bitter taste — and add the segments of fruit. When the temperature has dropped to about 70°F (21°C) add the enzymes and yeast, cover the bucket and strain after the initial head has subsided, place in a demijohn, top up to the neck of the bottle and fit an air lock.

Potato wine is one of the few wines that does benefit from the flavouring of demerara sugar, but if you wish to economise you may replace it with ordinary household sugar. It is best to use as highly flavoured raisins as possible, the large seedless type are ideal.

WHEAT AND POTATO WINE

This is another traditional wine in which crushed wheat is used to replace the raisins in the above recipe. Omit the pectic enzyme when making this wine.

SEVILLE ORANGE WINE

Not the cheapest of wines, but for anyone wishing to imitate a dry sherry, this wine is without peer. Unfortunately the fruit is only available in the shops for about a fortnight and the wine must be made during this time.

It is well worth asking your greengrocer if he has any marked fruit, which he is often glad to sell cheaper. This is ideal provided that you first discard any decayed parts of the fruit.

4 lb (2 kg) Seville oranges
½ lb (250 gm) sultanas
3 lb (1.5 kg) sugar
pectic enzyme
yeast

Peel the oranges, discard the skins and ensure that all the white pieces of pith are removed. Failure to do this will result in the wine having a bitter taste. Place the fruit segments in a bucket, break up either by hand or with a knife.

Add the minced sultanas, do not use raisins as the flavour tends to be overpowering. Add four pints (2 litres) of boiling water, allow to stand for half an hour, then add the sugar dissolved in two pints (1 litre) of water. When the mixture is tepid the yeast and pectic enzyme should be added. Stir thoroughly. When the initial fermentation has subsided, strain and transfer to a demijohn, top with water and fit an air lock. Rack, if heavy sediment has formed, after six weeks. When fermentation is complete transfer the liquid to two demijohns, so that they are half filled, cork and allow to stand for a fortnight in a cool place for the sherrying process to occur (note it is essential at this stage that the wine is free from all deposits). Recombining the two portions, bottle the wine, which may be drunk immediately.

SWEDE WINE

When making a swede wine it is important to use the large raisins, as these have a far better flavour than the smaller varieties.

3 lb (1.5 kg) swedes
1 lb (0.5 kg) raisins
2½ lb (1.25 kg) white sugar
½ lb (250 gm) demerara sugar
2 tsp citric acid
starch enzyme (amylase)
yeast

If the raisins contain any large stones, remove these before placing in the fermentation vessel. Peel, dice and place the swedes in a saucepan with two pints (1 litre) of water. Bring to the boil and simmer until soft. Strain the hot liquid on to the raisins. Add the demerara sugar and two pounds (1 kg) of white sugar. Provide two pints of hot water and stir until the sugar has dissolved. Make up to one gallon (4.5 litres). At 70°F (21°C) provide the acid, enzyme and yeast. After the initial fermentation has subsided strain and transfer to a demijohn. Ferment to dryness, feed with the remaining white sugar until a sweet high alcohol wine is obtained. Allow to mature for at least a year.

DRIED SLOE AND BANANA WINE

¼ lb (110 gm) dried sloes
1 lb (0.5 kg) bananas
1 lb (0.5 kg) crushed wheat
2¾ lb (1.4 kg) sugar
2 tsp citric acid
starch enzyme (amylase)
yeast

Cover both the dried sloes and the wheat with boiling water. Allow to stand in a covered container overnight. Extract the banana by simmering with a pint of water for twenty minutes. Strain the liquor into the fermenting bucket. Add the sugar and a further two pints (1 litre) of hot water. Stir until the sugar has dissolved. Make up to one gallon (4.5 litres). At the fermentation temperature provide the acid, amylase and yeast. Stir daily. Strain when the fermentation is at a controlled rate. Transfer to a demijohn. Rack as necessary. Mature for nine months to a year.

FIG AND ROSEHIPS

Utilise any remaining rosehips, either wild or cultivated, to make this tawny dessert wine.

2 lb (1 kg) crushed rosehips
½ lb (250 gm) dried figs
3 lb (1.5 kg) sugar
2 tsp citric acid
pectic enzyme
yeast

Remove all traces of stalk from the rosehips, then chop the figs into small pieces and place both in a bucket. Add the sugar and acid together with four pints (2 litres) of boiling water, stir until dissolved. Make up to one gallon (4.5 litres) with tap water, allow to cool to about 70°F (21°C) before adding the yeast and pectic enzyme. Stir daily. When the initial head has subsided, strain and transfer to a demijohn, topping up if necessary. If the wine is dry when fermentation ceases feed with two ounces (50 gm) portions of sugar until a sweet wine is obtained.

OTHER WINES TO MAKE DURING JANUARY

Grapefruit, pineapple, gooseberry, lychees, prune, bilberry, mixed fruit, raisin and banana (see February).
Tea, cranberry, dried elderberry, dried elderflower, dried orange blossom, dried peach, dried sloe, fig and banana (see March).
Orange, grapefruit, dried rosehip and banana (see April).
Ginger, banana (see May).
Rice, dried prune, dried date, dried apricot, dried apricot and banana, rosehip and parsnip, date and banana (see November).
Turnip, barley and potato, sultana, banana and elderflower (see December).

W·I·N·E·M·A·K·I·N·G M·O·N·T·H B·Y M·O·N·T·H
FEBRUARY

There are no fruits or vegetables, with the exception of parsnip and potato, from which wines can be made during this month. It is, however, an ideal time to make wines from canned and bottled fruits and fruit juices. Whilst these tend to be more expensive than those made from fresh fruit, they have the advantage of bearing the closest resemblance to commercial table wines. They are by far the easiest of all wines to make and have the shortest maturation period.

GOOSEBERRY WINE I

The easiest of all wines to make and for those who like a white table wine this is an absolute must.

16 oz (0.5 kg) tin gooseberries
½ tin white grape juice concentrate
2 lb (1.0 kg) sugar
6 drops of grape juice tannin
pectic enzyme
yeast

All the ingredients may be considered free of bacteria and the carbon dioxide generated during the initial fermentation will offer adequate protection from attack. Consequently there is no need to use boiling water which may destroy some of the compounds responsible for the more delicate fragrances of the grape juice.

The gooseberries, the syrup, the concentrate, tannin and sugar dissolved in a pint (0.5 litre) of luke warm water should be placed with four pints of water in a bucket 70°F (21°C). Add the yeast and pectic enzyme. Strain after a week, transfer to a demijohn and top up with water.

GOOSEBERRY WINE II

This gives a full bodied white dessert wine.

16 oz (0.5 kg) tin gooseberries
1 can white grape juice concentrate
1 lb (0.5 kg) sugar
1 lb (0.5 kg) bananas
6 drops of grape juice tannin
1 tsp citric acid
yeast

The wine is made as described for Gooseberry Wine I except that the juice of one pound (0.5 kg) of bananas is added, to give extra body. Peel the bananas, discard the skins, bring to the boil and simmer for twenty minutes. Allow to cool, gently squeeze it through the strainer and add to other ingredients. This, being a high alcohol wine, takes longer to ferment, and is seldom at its best until at least a year old. Extra sugar may be added to the finished wine.

EXOTIC FRUIT WINE

By using canned fruits and the lightly flavoured grape juice concentrate, it is possible to make a variety of delicate wines that retain, to a surprisingly high degree, the flavour and bouquet of a variety of exotic fruits. Whilst some of the wines may appear to possess only novelty value they are very distinctive and a great favourite with many.

16 oz (0.5 kg) tin of either pineapple, lychees, guavas or peaches
½ lb (250 gm) sugar
1 can white grape juice concentrate
6 drops of grape juice tannin
pectic enzyme
yeast

Place the ingredients together in a bucket and add the pectic enzyme and yeast when the temperature is 70°F (21°C) then make the total volume up to six pints (3 litres). Allow to ferment until the initial head has subsided. This will take from 5–10 days. Strain and transfer to a demijohn and finish in the usual way.

The finished wine should be medium sweet, if it ferments to dryness add sugar syrup to taste. Such wines are best drunk whilst still young.

GRAPEFRUIT WINE

19 oz (540 gm) tin grapefruit
1 lb (0.5 kg) sultanas
2 lb (1.0 kg) sugar
½ tsp citric acid
6 drops grape juice tannin
pectic enzyme
yeast

Mince the sultanas — do not use raisins as they are too highly flavoured — and cover in a bucket with two pints (1 litre) of boiling water. Add the sugar dissolved in a pint of water together with the grapefruit segments, the juice, tannin and 3 pints of water. Allow the temperature to reach 70°F (21°C), add the yeast and pectic enzyme. After a week strain into the demijohn, fill to the neck and fit an air lock. This wine will be ready for drinking in two months.

Half a can of grape juice concentrate may be used in place of the sultanas.

BILBERRY WINE I

16 oz (0.5 kg) bottle of bilberries
1 can white grape juice concentrate
½ lb (250 gm) sugar
pectic enzyme
yeast

You can often improve the quality of the wine made from grape juice concentrate by incorporating a small quantity of another ingredient. Such wines are more expensive than most country wines, but the increase in quality more than compensates for this.

Ignore the instructions given with the can of grape juice concentrate when making this wine. Place the bilberries, juice, sugar and the grape concentrate together with two pints (1 litre) of water in a bucket. Ferment on the must for the next ten days. Strain before transferring to a demijohn and topping up with water. Fit an air lock.

The resultant wine is a full bodied red table wine of surprisingly good quality that may be drunk after three months and goes on improving for at least two years.

BILBERRY WINE II

16 oz (0.5 kg) bottle of bilberries
1 lb (0.5 kg) light sultanas
2¼ lb (1.1 kg) sugar
1 tsp citric acid
pectic enzyme
yeast

Place the bilberries, juice, sugar and sultanas in a bucket. Add three pints (1.5 litres) of boiling water. Stir until the sugar has dissolved. Make up to one gallon (4.5 litres) with cold water. Add acid, yeast and pectic enzyme. Stir daily and proceed by the method given for bilberry wine above.

FRUIT JUICE WINES

Some of the easiest of all wines to make are those from fruit juices. Use the cans of unconcentrated juices available from supermarkets.

20 fl oz (0.5 litre) orange juice
1 lb (0.5 kg) sultanas
2¼ lb (1.25 kg) sugar
1 lb (0.5 kg) ripe bananas
1 tsp citric acid
pectic enzyme
yeast

Boil and simmer the peeled bananas for twenty minutes in one pint (0.5 litre) of water, strain and lightly squeeze. Add the liquid to the fruit juice, the sugar dissolved in two pints (1 litre) of water, the minced sultanas, the citric acid, and a further two pints (1 litre) of water. When the temperature is at 70°F (21°C) add the pectic enzyme and yeast and make up to one gallon (4.5 litres).

After a week, transfer to a demijohn, fit an air lock and ferment to dryness.

If the wine is made from grapefruit juice then omit the teaspoonful of citric acid.

The wine is even easier to make, though slightly more expensive, if you replace the sultanas with half a can of grape juice concentrate. All the ingredients may be put straight into the demijohn including the sugar and the acid, both of which may be dissolved in water. Use only the minimum amount of water to dissolve the sugar and ensure that the fermenting vessel is only three-quarters full, fit an air lock. Add the yeast and pectic enzyme and allow fermentation to proceed until the initial head has subsided, usually after about a week. Then top up with tap water and ferment in the usual way.

Alternatively, the sultanas in the above recipe may be replaced by a pint (0.5 litre) of white grape juice (not concentrate)). Using this ingredient it is not necessary to strain the must before placing in the demijohn. Minor variations in taste will result depending upon the source of the sultanas, grape juice concentrate or grape juice.

Variations
The orange juice may be replaced by either grapefruit or pineapple juice.

PRUNE WINE

Tinned prunes may be used to make a wine possessing many of the characteristics of a sweet sherry. Sherries are slightly oxidised and this effect can be simulated by allowing the wine to stand for a short period of time in a half filled container.

1 lb (0.5 kg) tin of prunes
1 lb (0.5 kg) sultanas
2 lb (1 kg) sugar
1 lb (0.5 kg) ripe bananas
1 tsp citric acid
glycerine
pectic enzyme
yeast

It is essential that the stones are removed from the prunes before they are added to the must, otherwise the wine will have a woody taste. Prepare the banana juice by boiling and simmering the peeled bananas for twenty minutes, when cool strain and lightly squeeze. Discard the pulp. Pour two pints (1 litre) of boiling water on to the minced sultanas, allow to stand for ten minutes, then add the juice from the bananas and one and a half pounds (0.75 kg) of sugar dissolved in two pints (1 litre) of water together with the stoned prunes, acid, yeast and enzyme. After the initial fermentation has ceased transfer to a demijohn, top up and fit an air lock. After the first heavy sediment has formed, rack and top up with the remaining half pound (250 gm) of sugar dissolved in sufficient water to refill the container. Allow fermentation to continue until no further bubbles escape from the air lock and the wine is clear. Transfer to two demijohns, half fill each, place corks in the tops, and store in a cool place for a fortnight.

   Bottle and add a tablespoonful of glycerine to each bottle. The wine is ready for drinking after another month and goes on improving for a year.

Variations
Replace the tin of prunes with half a pound (250 gm) of dried prunes. Pour sufficient boiling water on the prunes to cover the fruit. Remove the stones

from the fruit and use as described above. Using this recipe increase the sugar by 6 ounces (175 gm). This wine has a less pronounced flavour than the recipe given under November wines. A fuller flavour will be developed if an aromatic raisin such as Muscatel is employed instead of sultanas.

MIXED FRUIT WINE

Some of the best wines contain a mixture of fruit, this particular recipe can be made at any time of the year.

½ lb (250 gm) raisins
½ lb (250 gm) sultanas
1½ lb (0.75 kg) ripe bananas
2 medium sized oranges
1 lemon
2½ lb (1.25 kg) white sugar
pectic enzyme
yeast

Remove all traces of decay from the peeled bananas, then bring them to the boil with two pints (1 litre) of water. Simmer for twenty minutes. Strain the grey liquid into the bucket. Bring the dried fruit just to the boil with a pint (0.5 litre) of water. Add both solid and liquid to the banana liquor then provide sugar and juice of the oranges and lemon. Make up to one gallon (4.5 litres) with tap water. Stir, when the sugar has dissolved completely add the yeast and pectic enzyme. After seven days strain, transfer to a demijohn and fit an airlock. The resultant medium wine is ready for drinking after six months.

PRUNE AND PARSNIP WINE

Both of the main ingredients of this wine possess a sherry type flavour, by combining them it is possible to develop a cream sherry style without employing an oxidation stage.

½ lb (250 gm) prunes
2 lb (1 kg) parsnips
3 lb (1.5 kg) sugar
2 tsp citric acid
starch enzyme (amylase)
pectic enzyme
yeast

Scrub but do not peel the parsnips, dice, place in the saucepan with two pints (1 litre) of water and simmer until soft. Pour the liquid and the solid on to the prunes. Add the sugar together with a further three pints (1.5 litres) of boiling water. Stir until all of the sugar has dissolved then add the citric acid. Make up to a gallon (4.5 litres) by adding tap water. At 65–70°F (18.5–21°C) provide both of the enzymes and the yeast. Stir daily; after the initial fermentation has ceased strain, place in a demijohn, top up and provide an airlock. Ferment and rack in the usual manner. If necessary feed with extra sugar to increase the degree of sweetness. The body and the sweetness of the wine may be improved by the addition of a tablespoonful of glycerine per bottle.

RAISIN AND BANANA WINE

The final taste of the wine will depend upon the type of raisins used. Try to obtain Muscatel or other sweet scented raisins.

1 lb (0.5 kg) raisins
2 lb (1 kg) bananas
2¾ lb (1.4 kg) sugar
2 tsp citric acid
yeast

As the raisins are moderately highly flavoured a total extraction of the bananas may be employed. Bring the peeled bananas just to the boil in sufficient water to cover them. Simmer for 20-30 minutes. Then pour the liquid and solid on to the raisins. Dissolve the sugar in about 5 pints (2.5 litres) of warm water and add the solution to the bucket. At 70°F (21°C) add the acid and yeast.

After seven days or when the vigorous head has subsided (whichever is the sooner), strain into a demijohn.

The degree of sweetness will depend upon the amount of sugar in the bananas and raisins, both of which may vary considerably. The wine is at its best if drunk as a medium sweet. Feed with extra sugar if necessary until this stage is reached.

The wine should be kept for at least nine months and is not at its best until it is eighteen months old.

OTHER WINES TO MAKE DURING FEBRUARY

Parsnip, potato, carrot, wheat and potato, fig and rosehip, dried sloe and banana, swede (see January)

Tea, cranberry, dried elderberry, dried elderflower, dried orange blossom, fig and banana, dried peach, dried sloe (see March)

Orange, grapefruit, dried rosehip and banana (see April)

Ginger, banana (see May)

Rice, dried prune, dried date, dried apricot (see November)

Dried apricot and banana, date and banana, sultana, banana and elderflower, turnip, barley and potato (see December)

W·I·N·E·M·A·K·I·N·G M·O·N·T·H B·Y M·O·N·T·H
MARCH

There are still very few fresh materials available during March, the only truly seasonal being birch sap. However, stocks of wine may be replenished by using dried and frozen materials.

BIRCH SAP WINE

This is unique amongst country wines in that all the liquid required is obtained from the main ingredient.

During the 2nd–4th weeks of March, the sap is rising in the birch trees. Check the tree by breaking a twig, if it is moist, a gallon (4.5 litres), but no more, of the sap can be safely taken without damaging the tree. Cut a circle an inch (2.5 cm) in diameter and extending two inches (5 cm) into the trunk about two foot (60 cm) from the base of the tree.

Fit a ¼ inch (0.5 cm) piece of glass tubing inserted into an inch (2.5 cm) cork as a bung and connected to rubber tubing into the hole and allow to drain into a covered pot. After about a gallon (4.5 litres) of the liquid has been collected, dismantle the apparatus and re-insert the plug in the tree. This will stop the tree bleeding, which could kill it, and the plug will be easily removed again next year.

1 gallon (4.5 litres) birch sap
1 lb (0.5 kg) sultanas
2½ lb (1.25 kg) sugar
1½ tsp citric acid
yeast

Dissolve the sugar by gently warming in three pints (1.5 litres) of birch sap. Add the citric acid and the sultanas, which should have previously been sterilised by covering with boiling water and discarding the sterilising water. At 70°F (21°C) add the yeast and ferment out in the usual way, straining after a week.

This gives a light crisp wine with a subtle but distinct flavour.

Variations
Replace the sultanas with a pint (0.5 litre) of white grape juice (not concentrate). This will allow you to omit the sterilising stage providing you have sterilised all of the equipment used in collecting the sap. There is also no need to strain the wine before placing in the demijohn.

Sycamore wine or walnut wine is made by the same method and either sultanas or grape juice can be used with the corresponding sap.

TEA WINE

¼ lb (100 gm) tea
2 lb (1 kg) sultanas or raisins
2 tsp citric acid or 4 oranges
2½ lb (1.25 kg) sugar
yeast

Although many recipes advocate using tea leaves which have already been infused or the liquid straight from the pot, this is a false economy as the resulting wine has a 'stewed' taste. Mince the raisins or sultanas and cover with boiling water. Add the sugar, dissolved in three pints (1.5 litres) of water and the citric acid and place together with the tea, prepared in the usual way, in a bucket. Make the total volume up to one gallon (4.5 litres) and when the temperature is at 70°F (21°C) add the yeast. Strain after one week. Transfer to a demijohn, fit an air lock and ferment to dryness.

Tea is very high in tannin and consequently the wine is not ready for drinking until it is at least a year old. It is a very good wine, with a distinctive flavour quite unreminiscent of tea. If you wish you can replace the citric acid with the juice from four medium sized oranges, ensuring that none of the pith from the fruit is allowed to enter the must.

A wine results which is considered by many to be even better than that made from citric acid.

Variation
The addition of half an ounce (15 gm) of either dried elderflowers or orange blossom greatly improves the bouquet of the wine.

Alternatively place the petals from two medium sized elderflower heads in the bucket with the sultanas. If using elderflowers it is important to read the instructions given for the use of this ingredient under June recipes.

DRIED ELDERBERRY

Elderberries produce one of the finest wines that we can make and, if you wish to build up your stocks of light dry table wine, dried elderberries can be used at any time of the year. However, if you do not dry your own berries, which can be done in the oven, this can work out expensive, so in order to cut your costs you may, by using the same berries twice, make two gallons (9 litres) of wine from each pound (0.5 kg) of dried berries.

First Gallon

1 lb (0.5 kg) dried elderberries
2½ lb (1.25 kg) sugar
2 tsp citric acid
yeast

Place the elderberries in a bucket with boiling water, add the sugar dissolved in two pints (1 litre) of water and the citric acid. Adjust the volume to six pints (3 litres) and when the temperature is at 70°F (21°C) add the yeast.

After two days (but no longer) strain off the liquid and transfer to a demijohn, fit an air lock without topping up the liquid level which should be done after the vigorous fermentation has died down (usually after a further 5–10 days) and there is no danger of the liquid overflowing. Retain the part-spent elderberries for making the second gallon, which to avoid any danger of infection, should be started immediately the berries are strained from the must.

If you prefer a wine with a little more body include either half a pound (250 gm) of sultanas or the juice obtained by simmering a pound (0.5 kg) of bananas for twenty minutes in 2 pints (1 litre) of water.

When adding the juice from the bananas adjust the volume of water accordingly.

Second Gallon

Part-spent elderberries
1 lb (0.5 kg) raisins
2½ lb (1.25 kg) sugar
2 tsp citric acid
pectic enzyme
yeast

Since much of the goodness will have been leached from the berries it is necessary to add raisins to the second batch and pectic enzyme to completely break the fruit down. You may, if you wish to give the wine extra body, add the juice obtained by boiling one and a half pounds (0.75 kg) of peeled bananas, but this is by no means essential as the wine is best drunk as a light dry table wine.

Cover the elderberries and minced raisins with four pints (2 litres) of boiling water, and add the sugar dissolved in two pints (1 litre) of water. If you are adding banana juice, it should be incorporated at this stage. Adjust the volume to one gallon (4.5 litres). Allow the temperature to drop to 70°F (21°C) and add the yeast and pectic enzyme. Strain the liquid and transfer to a demijohn after five days, but under no circumstances any longer as elderberries are so high in tannin that the resultant wine would be undrinkable for several years. Then ferment to dryness.

When fermentation has ceased, mix the two batches of wine and allow a year to mature.

DRIED ELDERFLOWER WINE

With the rapid increase in the popularity of home winemaking, it is possible to buy a wide variety of specially prepared ingredients. As these tend to make the hobby expensive, only those that produce the very best wines are worth considering. Perhaps the finest of all the true country wines is elderflower and this can be made at any time of the year by using dried flowers.

2 oz (50 gm) dried elderflowers
1 lb (0.5 kg) sultanas
2½ lb (1.25 kg) sugar
2 tsp citric acid
pectic enzyme
yeast

Pour two pints (1 litre) of boiling water on to the dried elderflowers and the minced sultanas (do not use raisins as the flavour is too strong). Add the sugar dissolved in two pints (1 litre) of water and the citric acid.

Adjust the volume to six pints (3 litres) and when the temperature has dropped to 70°F (21°C) add the yeast and the pectic enzyme. Strain after a week, transfer to a demijohn, top up with water and ferment to dryness.

ORANGE BLOSSOM WINE

Use the method and recipe given above, replacing the elderflowers with an equal amount of orange blossom petals.

DRIED PEACH WINE

Dried fruit may be used for winemaking provided that the fruit has been soaked in boiling water prior to fermenting.

½ lb (250 gm) dried peaches
1 lb (0.5 kg) sultanas
1 lb (0.5 kg) bananas
2¼ lb (1.1 kg) sugar
2 tsp citric acid
pectic enzyme
wine yeast

Place the peaches and sultanas in a fermenting bucket, add four pints (2 litres) of boiling water and allow to stand for four hours. Then add the pectic enzyme. Allow to stand under a tight fitting lid. Next day simmer the peeled bananas with a pint (0.5 litre) of water for twenty minutes. Strain the liquid into the fermenting bucket. Add the acid and sugar, stir until the solids have dissolved, then make the total volume up to one gallon (4.5 litres). Add the yeast. Keep the must at 65–70°F (18.5–21°C). After a fortnight strain into a demijohn and fit an airlock. Depending upon the fermentation temperature the wine should be ready for drinking from six months onwards.

FROZEN CRANBERRY WINE

Frozen fruits are another source of ingredients that the home winemaker can use all the year round. Some fruits such as cranberries are usually only available frozen and this adds another dimension to the hobby.

1 lb (0.5 kg) frozen cranberries
1½ lb (0.75 kg) sultanas
2 lb (1 kg) sugar
1½ tsp citric acid
pectic enzyme
yeast

Place the minced sultanas in a bucket and cover with two pints (1 litre) of boiling water, add the sugar dissolved in two pints (1 litre) of water and the citric acid. In a separate sterilised container cover the cranberries with boiling water, then thoroughly mash the fruit with a fork. Pour the resultant slurry into the bucket with the other ingredients. When the temperature has reached 70°F (21°C) add the yeast and the pectic enzyme. After the initial head has subsided transfer to a demijohn, top up and fit an air lock. This produces a light rosè wine delicious with most meals.

Variations
Replace the sultanas with a 1¾ pint (1 litre) carton of apple juice. Because of the ease of oxidation of apples, place the cranberries, sugar and apple juice in the bucket, make up to one gallon (4.5 litres) and add a Campden tablet.

Add a vigorously working yeast starter. Immediately after the final racking add one Campden tablet. Alternatively this wine can be made as a semi-sparkling rosè, in which case you should omit the final, but not the first, Campden tablet. Rack the wine into champagne bottles, add half a teaspoonful of sugar, cork and wire down as described under sparkling wines. Leave at fermentation temperature for one month, after which time the wine may be served, chilled.

FIG AND BANANA WINE

½ lb (250 gm) dried figs
2 lb (1 kg) bananas
2½ lb (1.25 kg) sugar
2 tsp citric acid
pectic enzyme
yeast

Use a slab of dried figs and cut each fruit in half; skin the ripe bananas and place in a bucket. Add half a gallon (2 litres) of boiling water, stir in the sugar and cool by adding a further two and a half pints (1.25 litres) of cold water. Allow the mixture to cool to the fermenting temperature, before adding the acid, pectic enzyme and wine yeast. Stir daily. After seven days (do not delay the next stage further with these strong flavoured ingredients) strain into a demijohn. Fit an airlock, rack when fermentation ceases.

The large variation in the sugar present in these fruits makes it impossible to predict exactly the final taste, which should be medium sweet; so if necessary feed the wine with two ounce aliquots of sugar. Some people prefer this heavily maderised wine after the addition of a tablespoon of glycerine per bottle.

DRIED SLOE WINE

Another ingredient which is dried and sold for winemaking is sloes. These are high in tannin and flavour but they are low in body and vinosity providing components, but they are extremely useful as part of a compound recipe.

¼ lb (100 gm) dried sloes
½ lb (250 gm) raisins
¼ lb (100 gm) dried pale malt extract
2¾ lb (1.4 kg) sugar
2 tsp citric acid
pectic enzyme
yeast

Soak the sloes, overnight, in a pint (0.5 litre) of boiling water. Place the reconstituted sloes and water into the fermenting vessel. Bring the raisins just to the boil with a pint (0.5 litre) of water. Transfer to the bucket. Dissolve the sugar and malt in four pints (2 litres) of hot water, add to the other ingredients and make the total volume up to one gallon (4.5 litres). Provide the acid, yeast and pectic enzyme, stir daily. Strain after seven to ten days. Ferment until the evolution of bubbles ceases or a quarter to half an inch of sediment forms, whichever is the sooner. Rack. Finish in the usual manner. This medium sweet wine which may be fed and sweetened if preferred is best allowed to mature for at least one year.

OTHER WINES TO MAKE DURING MARCH

Parsnip, potato, wheat and potato, dried sloe and banana, swede (see January)
Grapefruit, prune, gooseberry, bilberry, pineapple, lychees, bilberry, mixed fruit, raisin and banana, prune and parsnip (see February)
Grapefruit, orange, dried rosehip and banana (see April)
Ginger, banana (see May)
Rice, dried prune, dried date, dried apricot, dried apricot and banana, date and banana, sultanas, banana and elderflower (see November)
Turnip, barley and potoato (see December)

W·I·N·E·M·A·K·I·N·G M·O·N·T·H B·Y M·O·N·T·H

APRIL

The winemaker's year really begins in April with the appearance of the first of the suitable flowers. Flowers provide only the bouquet of a wine and all flower wines are simply flavoured sultana wines — never use raisins as their strong flavour will override that of the flowers. Nevertheless many consider these unsurpassable for light luncheon wines. When collecting flowers for wine always ensure that they are gathered away from the main roads otherwise your drink will taste of diesel oil. Where quantities of flowers are quoted they refer to the volume when the heads, the only part required, are lightly pressed down.

DANDELION WINE

To make dandelion wine you will require about four pints (2 litres) of heads, and although the plant seems to flower in our lawns all the year around, they will only be available in sufficient quantities for winemaking for a fortnight in the middle of April, the exact time depending upon your locality.

2 quarts (2 litres) dandelion heads
1½ lb (0.75 kg) sultanas
2½ lb (1.25 kg) sugar
4 oranges
6 drops of grape juice tannin
or 1 cup of tea (no milk)
yeast

Wash the flowers and ensure that they are free from insects. Make sure that all the stems are removed from the heads, otherwise it will give the wine a bitter taste. Place the flower heads, minced sultanas, sugar and the juice from the oranges in a bucket and cover with six pints (3 litres) of boiling water. Do not worry about the boiling water destroying the bouquet as some authorities state — this is a fallacy. When the mixture has cooled to 70°F (21°C) add the yeast and tannin or cold tea. Stir daily. Do not be perturbed by the strong distinctly unpleasant smell at this stage, it will disappear. Once experimenting with this recipe I boiled the dandelions, and on walking into the kitchen discovered why the country name for these flowers is 'pee in the bed'.

After a week transfer to a demijohn, top up, fit an air lock. Rack when the first heavy sediment occurs.

Variations
The same basic recipes are applicable to all flower wines and the dandelions may be replaced with the same quantity of coltsfoot gorse or broom flowers.

USING GRAPEJUICE

Replace the sultans with two pints (1 litre) of white grape juice. This will allow you to omit the straining stage. Place the petals in a suitable sized muslin bag, with a string attached. Cover the bag with two pints (1 litre) of boiling water. Allow to cool before adding the grape juice, sugar dissolved in two pints of water and the juice of the oranges. Make up to one gallon (4.5 litres) and proceed as above. Remove the flowers after three days, this produces a subtler flavour consistent with that of the grape juice. Transfer without straining to a demijohn when the initial head has subsided.

COLTSFOOT WINE

This flower produces a wine very similar to that obtained from dandelions in the previous recipe, or if you prefer a fuller sweet wine you may use this variation.

2 quarts (2 litres) coltsfoot
2 lb (1 kg) sultanas
1½ lb (0.75 kg) bananas
2 lb (1 kg) sugar
2 tsp citric acid
6 drops of grape juice tannin
or 1 cup cold tea (no milk)
yeast

Thoroughly clean the flowers, remove any trace of stalk and place in a bucket with the minced sultanas and one and a half pounds (0.75 kilo) of the sugar, cover with four pints (2 litres) of boiling water. Add the juice obtained from boiling the peeled bananas with two pints (1 litre) of water for twenty minutes and strain. Make up the volume to one gallon (4.5 litres) and when tepid add the yeast and the grape juice tannin or cold tea.

Allow to ferment in the bucket for ten days, stirring each day, then transfer to the demijohn, top up if necessary, and fit an air lock.

When the first heavy sediment forms, rack and make up the volume with the remaining half pound (250 gm) of sugar dissolved in the minimum amount of water. Allow fermentation to proceed until no further bubbles escape from the air lock. At this stage the wine should still be sweet. If it is not, rack it and add another quarter of a pound (100 gm) of sugar and return to the fermentation cabinet. Extra body can be given to the wine by the addition of a tablespoonful of glycerine per bottle.

If you wish, you can use a similar quantity of dandelions, gorse of broom instead of coltsfoot.

Variations
Coltsfoot wine may be made using white grape juice according to the method given on page 66.

GORSE OR BROOM WINE

White grape juice concentrate can be used in conjunction with flowers to produce subtle wines that have more character than the concentrates do on their own. Use a full can marketed for making one gallon (4.5 litres) of wine and taste the difference when you add these extra ingredients.

Gorse is in flower all the year round — as the old country saying states 'when gorse is not in flower, kissing is out of season'.

But the disadvantage of using gorse is the spines encountered when picking the flowers. Broom does not have this disadvantage and it makes an almost identical wine, but it has only a limited flowering period.

2 quarts (2 litres) of gorse or broom flowers
1 tin grape juice concentrate
¾ lb (350 gm) sugar
2 oranges
4 drops grape juice tannin
yeast

Grape juice concentrate comes complete with instructions, ignore them when making this wine.

Use only the yellow leguminous flowers, removing all green material. Thoroughly wash and cover the flowers with four pints (2 litres) of boiling water, add the sugar as a solid and the juice from the two medium sized oranges. Allow the liquid to cool to 70°F (21°C); add the grape juice concentrate, washing the final traces from the tin with a small quantity of warm water. Add the yeast and grape juice tannin. Finish in the usual way to produce a medium dry wine.

Variation
Gorse and broom wine may be made using white grape juice according to the method given on page 66.

CYSER

Honey although expensive makes some of the most interesting of wines, which some people prefer to the usual sugar-based country wines. When using honey, due to the presence of pollen (which can cause problems with clarity) and the very real danger of vinegaring and off-flavours due to the micro-organisms that are always present, it is necessary to boil the honey before fermenting. It is also advisable to use yeast nutrient with any style of mead. Cyser is a ferment of honey and apple juice and whilst this was always made in the autumn in the natural season of the ingredients, today it is possible to make it at any time of the year.

> *2 pints (1 litre) apple juice*
> *2 lb (1 kg) light honey*
> *1 lb (0.5 kg) sugar*
> *1 tsp citric or tartaric acid*
> *cup of cold tea (without milk)*
> *yeast nutrient*
> *pectic enzyme*
> *yeast*

Pour the honey and two pints (1 litre) of water into the saucepan and with constant stirring bring to the boil. Skim off and discard any scum that appears on the top of the liquid. Pour into the fermenting bucket, add the apple juice, the cup of cold tea and the sugar dissolved in a pint (0.5 litre) of water. Make up to one gallon (4.5 litres) with cold tap water, bring the temperature to 65-70°F (18.5-21°C). Add the yeast, nutrient, acid and enzyme. Stir the must daily. Immediately the initial fermentation ceases transfer to a demijohn, top up and fit an airlock. All honey-based drinks are prone to oxidation, so ensure that the wine never comes into contact with excess air. Rack and top up as required. The wine which will be dry to medium dry benefits from keeping for at least a year and may be drunk as an aperitif, with a meal or simply enjoyed on its own.

ORANGE WINE

8 oranges (medium sized)
1 lb (0.5 kg) sultanas
1½ lb (0.75 kg) bananas
3 lb (1.5 kg) sugar
9 drops of grape juice tannin
pectic enzyme
yeast

When making wine from oranges it is essential to use only the juice, any pith present will give the wine a bitter taste. Any of the patent citrus fruit extractors may be used, or the fruit can be peeled taking care to clean off all the white pieces, and the segments placed in a liquidiser.

Cover the minced sultanas, two and a half pounds (1.25 kg) of the sugar and the orange juice with four pints (2 litres) of boiling water. Stir thoroughly to dissolve the sugar. Add the juice obtained from straining and slightly squeezing the bananas after simmering in a pint (0.5 litre) of water for twenty minutes. Make the mixture up to a gallon (4.5 litres) and when the temperature is at 70°F (21°C) add the yeast, pectic enzyme and the grape juice tannin.

Rack after the first heavy sediment, and make up the volume with the remaining half pound (250 gm) of sugar dissolved in the minimum quantity of water. When fermentation is complete the wine should be medium sweet. Extra sugar syrup can be added to taste.

GRAPEFRUIT WINE

Many of the finest table wines possess a bouquet faintly reminiscent of citrus fruit, this can be imitated by making a wine from grapefruit.

3 medium sized grapefruit
15 oz (0.5 kg) tin gooseberries
2 lb (1 kg) sugar
12 drops of grape juice tanin
pectic enzyme
yeast

This wine should be devoid of any brown coloration, consequently sultanas or raisins cannot be used and bananas tend to give an overpowering flavour, for this reason tinned gooseberries, another excellent ingredient for giving body to a wine, must be incorporated.

Juice the grapefruit, ensuring that no pith is associated with the liquid. Place with the gooseberries and the syrup in a bucket. Add the sugar dissolved in two pints (1 litre) of water, the grape juice tannin solution, the pectic enzyme and yeast. Make up to one gallon.

After four days the initial head should have subsided (leave longer if this is not the case) strain and lightly squeeze the fruit pulp and transfer to a demijohn. Fill to the top and fit an air lock. For this wine to retain its delicate colour it is essential that a Campden tablet is added after racking which should be performed immediately fermentation ceases.

This is a very fine dry table wine.

DRIED ROSEHIP AND BANANA

3 lb (1.5 kg) bananas
½ lb (250 gm) dried rosehips
½ lb (250 gm) raisins
2½ lb (1.25 kg) white sugar
½ lb (250 gm) demerara sugar
2 tsp citric acid
yeast

Place the rosehips and the raisins in a bowl, cover with a pint (0.5 litre) of boiling water and allow to stand overnight. Remove the skins and any decayed material from the bananas, break up and place in a bucket. Add half a gallon (2 litres) of boiling water, the reconstituted dried fruit and the liquid together with two pounds (1 kg) of white sugar, all the demerara sugar and the acid. Make up to one gallon (4.5 litres) at 70°F (21°C), add the yeast, stir daily. When the initial fermentation has subsided, strain and transfer to a demijohn. Ferment and rack as necessary. When the wine is dry feed with 4 oz (110 gm) of white sugar. Repeat if necessary. Allow this tawny dessert wine to keep for at least one year before drinking.

Variation
Replace the banana with half a pound (225 gm) of sultanas. Treat the sultanas by the same method as is employed with the other dried fruit.

ORANGE MELOMEL

Melomels are ferments made from honey and fruit juices and were probably the first true country wines, as it seems that the idea of making alcoholic drinks from wild fruits predates the arrival of sugar in this country. Since honey contains 87 per cent sugar it may be used to replace this ingredient in any recipe, yet in all but the most suitable of complementary flavours the expense cannot be really justified. Due to the extreme delicacy of the honey flavour it is better to use pre-extracted fruit juices than to attempt to do it yourself. As an economy one part of sugar to two parts of honey is used. If you have access to honey supplies you may like to replace the sugar with a corresponding amount of honey.

2 pints (1 litre) pure orange juice
2 lb (1 kg) light honey
1 lb (0.5 kg) sugar
1 tsp citric or tartaric acid
cup of cold tea
yeast nutrient
wine yeast

Pour the honey into a saucepan with two pints (1.0 litre) of tap water, bring just to the boil and skim off the scum which forms. Transfer to the bucket, add the sugar, the cup of cold tea and a further two pints (1 litre) of hot water, stir until dissolved. Partially cool the mixture by the addition of a pint (0.5 litre) of cold tap water before adding the orange juice, then provide the yeast nutrient, acid and wine yeast at 70°F (21°C). Stir or shake daily. As soon as the initial ferment subsides transfer to a demijohn and immediately top up with tap water. Fermentation should cease when the wine is medium dry. Drink whilst still fresh, that is after six to nine months.

PYMENT

Pyment is the name given to any ferment of grape juice and honey. It may be considered as a specialist type of melomel and is made by replacing the orange juice with 20 fl oz (0.5 litre) of grape juice and increasing the acid to one and a half teaspoonfuls and the cold tap water to two pints (1 litre).

OTHER WINES TO MAKE DURING APRIL

Potato, wheat and potato, dried sloe and banana (see January)
Grapefruit, prune, gooseberry, bilberry, pineapple, lychees, mixed fruit, raisin and banana, prune and parsnip (see February)
Tea, cranberry, dried elderberry, dried elderflower, dried orange blossom, dried peach, dried sloe, fig and banana (see March)
Ginger, banana (see May)

Rice, dried prune, dried date, dried apricot and banana, date and banana (see November)
Barley and potato, sultana, banana and elderflower (see December)

W·I·N·E·M·A·K·I·N·G M·O·N·T·H B·Y M·O·N·T·H

MAY

There is still not a great deal of fresh material available for winemaking. But rhubarb and some herbs are coming into season and by the end of the month the first elderflowers are beginning to appear and there are usually enough gorse and broom flowers about if you missed them during April.

RHUBARB WINE

This is a wine that should not be omitted from your cellar, for not only is it very cheap to make, but it has a unique flavour of its own which is extremely pleasant.

Depending upon the variety, fresh growths of rhubarb occur throughout the summer months. Provided that you use only young sticks, older sticks tend to be far too high in acid, it is possible to make the wine throughout the summer.

3 lb (1.5 kg) rhubarb
3 lb (1.5 kg) sugar
yeast

In order to remove the excess acid from the rhubarb it is necessary to soak the fruit for one month. To avoid the danger of infection it is essential to use a bucket with an airtight lid or you may use a plastic bucket covered with a plastic film.

Cut the rhubarb into pieces about two inches (5 cm) in length (do not peel) and place in a bucket with six pints (3 litres) of boiling water, cover with lid. After a month a white scum develops, remove and then strain into another bucket squeezing the remains of the rhubarb gently. Add the sugar and yeast, stir and leave in the bucket for a further week, then transfer to a demijohn, top up, fit an air lock and ferment to dryness.

RHUBARB AND ELDERFLOWER

The elderflowers will not be available until next month, but since this is a variation on rhubarb wine it will be considered here.

Prepare rhubarb wine as described above, but instead of adding six pints (3 litres) of boiling water reduce this amount by one pint (0.5 litre).

Prior to adding the sugar and yeast, place the flowering heads from four medium sized flowers, in a muslin bag, fitted with a string, in a pan. Cover with a pint (0.5 litre) of boiling water. Leave for half an hour. Add the liquid and the bag to the rhubarb. Add the sugar and the yeast. Remove the bag after three days. Then proceed as described above.

Variation

This makes an ideal sparkling wine. When the wine is dry, bottle in champagne bottles and add half a teaspoonful of sugar to each bottle, cork and wire down as described on page 31. Then place at fermentation temperature for one month and leave to mature for a further three months.

NETTLE WINE

This is one of the better herb wines.

4 pints (2 litres) of nettle heads
1 lb (0.5 kg) sultanas
2 lb (1 kg) sugar
2 tsp citric acid
yeast

Pick the top two inches (5 cm) of the nettles, whilst the growth is still young, clean the nettles and place in a bucket with the sugar, the minced sultanas and the citric acid. Add six pints (3 lites) of boiling water. Allow to cool and add the yeast. Stir daily. Ferment on the must for one week but no longer and finish the wine in the usual way.

BRAMBLE TIP WINE

Another example of a true country wine, made from the ingredients of the hedgerow. Being only lightly flavoured and low in alcohol it makes an excellent table wine.

4 pints (2 litres) bramble tips
1 lb (0.5 kg) sultanas
2 lb (1 kg) sugar
1½ tsp citric acid
yeast

Pick only the leading two inches (5 cm) of the new bramble tips, just as the buds are bursting and make the wine by the method given for nettle wine.

WALLFLOWER WINE

Wallflowers are amongst the strongest scented of all flowers and consequently only a small quantity of the petals are required to make a delicately scented wine. If you use the light coloured petals you will obtain a white to golden wine whilst the darker coloured petals produce a most delicate pink wine. The taste is identical in both cases.

1 large cupful wallflower petals
1 lb (0.5 kg) light coloured sultanas
2¾ lb (1.4 kg) sugar
2 tsp citric acid or 2 lemons
pectic enzyme
wine yeast

Gather the petals on a warm day when they are emitting the maximum perfume. Remove all green and extraneous material. Use immediately. Place the sultanas, acid (or the juice of two lemons) and sugar in the bucket. Cover with four pints (2 litres) boiling water. Leave for twenty minutes and add a further three pints (1.5 litres) of water at tap temperature. Check that the temperature is in the range 65-70°F (18.5–21°C) before adding the yeast and pectic enzyme. Stir daily. After seven to ten days, strain, transfer to a demijohn and top up if necessary. Rack as required. Drink after six months.

Variation

1 large cupful wallflower petals
1 can white grape juice concentrate
1 cup of cold tea (without milk)
10 oz (270 gm) sugar
wine yeast

Adopt the method given above with the exception that the wallflowers should be covered with a pint (0.5 litre) of boiling water. Add the sugar, stir until dissolved. Add four pints (2 litres) of cold water, make up to one gallon

(4.5 litres) with the grape juice concentrate, washings from the can, cold tea and tap water. Add yeast and ferment as described above.
NOTE: In some parts of the country, wallflowers are known as gillies and this is also referred to as gillies wine.

HAWTHORN BLOSSOM WINE

Hawthorn or May Blossom appears at the end of the month, and may be used to make a wine with a very unique bouquet. Since the flower is more strongly scented than dandelions a smaller quantity of blossoms must be used.

2 pints (1 litre) hawthorn blossom
1½ lb (0.75 kg) sultanas
2½ lb (1.25 kg) sugar
4 oranges
6 drops of grape juice tannin
or 1 cup of cold tea (no milk)
pectic enzyme
yeast

Make this wine by the method given for dandelion wine.
Alternatively if you like a sweeter wine you can substitute two pints (1 litre) of hawthorn blossom for the four pints (2 litres) of coltsfoot in the coltsfoot wine recipe. Hawthorn has too sweet a bouquet to really complement the subtle flavour of grape juice concentrate and it is not recommended that you use the method given under gorse blossom for this particular flower.

BANANA WINE

Banana wine is a very full bodied wine that retains a very strong banana bouquet and flavour. If you do not like this flavour then this is not the wine for you. It can be a very cheap wine if you ask your greengrocer for over-ripe bananas which are ideal for our purpose and are often sold very cheaply.

4 lb (2 kg) bananas (unpeeled weight)
2½ lb (1.25 kg) sugar
2½ tsp citric acid
12 drops of grape juice tannin
or 1 cup of cold tea (no milk)
pectic enzyme
yeast

Discard the peel and remove any decayed fruit, place in a saucepan with enough water to cover and a little in excess, bring to the boil and simmer for about twenty minutes with the lid on the saucepan. When the fruit is soft enough, mash thoroughly and allow to cool. Strain the liquid, which will be a very unappetising greyish white, on to the sugar. Add the citric acid and tannin and allow to cool before the addition of pectic enzyme and yeast. The liquid can immediately be transferred to a demijohn (it will come to no harm if left in the bucket for a week but no longer), and the total volume made up to six pints (3 litres). Provide the yeast and pectic enzyme. After a further week the demijohn should be topped up. Finish the wine by keeping warm, until the bubbles escape from the air lock.

This wine will be sweet provided that there is sufficient residual sugar in the bananas. If the wine is not sweet enough add sugar to taste.

GINGER WINE

1 oz (25 gm) root ginger
1½ lb (0.75 kg) sultanas
2 lb (1.0 kg) sugar
1½ tsp citric acid
pectic enzyme
yeast

Hammer the root ginger, cover with two pints (1 litre) of boiling water and decant the liquid after half an hour. Add to the sugar, minced sultanas and citric acid. Add a further four pints (2 litres) of boling water, stir thoroughly to dissolve the sugar, allow to cool then add the pectic enzyme and the yeast. After a fortnight strain, transfer to a demijohn, top up, fit an air lock and ferment to dryness.

There is no general agreement as to what constitutes the best ginger wine. Adjust the wine to suit your palate, sweeten with sugar syrup if you wish. If you prefer a stronger ginger flavour, soak the root ginger for an hour but no longer.

PRIMROSE WINE

This was once one of the most popular of country wines, but it is rarely encountered today due to the large number of petals of this increasingly scarce plant that is required. Should you possess a private supply of this flower (never gather the wild blooms) use the recipe given for wallflowers, replacing the cupful of petals with a pint of primrose blossom.

COWSLIP OR OXSLIP WINE

As for primrose wine.

OTHER WINES TO MAKE DURING MAY

Potato, fig and rosehip, dried sloe and banana (see January)
Grapefruit, prune, gooseberry, bilberry, pineapple, lychees, mixed fruit, raisin and banana (see February)
Tea, cranberry, dried elderberry, dried elderflower, dried orange blossom, dried peach, fig and banana, dried sloe (see March)
Grapefruit, orange, dandelion, broom, gorse, coltsfoot, dried rosehip and banana (see April)
Rhubarb champagne (see July)
Rice, dried prune, dried date, dried apricot, dried apricot and banana, date and banana (see November)
Sultanas, banana and elderflower (see December)

W·I·N·E·M·A·K·I·N·G M·O·N·T·H B·Y M·O·N·T·H
JUNE

June sees the beginning of the season which is the busiest in the winemaker's year, fresh fruits are just beginning to come into season and the elderflowers are at their peak.

ELDERFLOWER WINE

This is one of the most popular of country wines, and if correctly made is one of the best. Pick the flowers on a fine day and carefully smell them to ensure that they have not got a catty bouquet, as this will come through in the finished wine, select only those flowers whose bouquet is slightly reminiscent of bananas.

TRADITIONAL COUNTRY ELDERFLOWER WINE

12 medium sized elderflowers
1 lb (0.5 kg) sultanas
2½ lb (1.25 kg) sugar
2 tsp citric acid
pectic enzyme
yeast

Medium sized flower heads are those which are about three inches (8 cm) across. If different sized heads are picked adjust the amount accordingly. Place the flower heads in a plastic bag, tie top and leave in the freezing cabinet of the refrigerator. Leave for two days. Remove the bag and shake. The petals will now separate from the green flower stalks that should be discarded.

Cover the petals and the minced sultanas with four pints (2 litres) of boiling water, stir in the sugar until dissolved and add the citric acid. Make the volume up to one gallon (4.5 litres) and when the temperature is about 70°F (21°C) add the yeast and the pectic enzyme. When the initial fermentation has subsided, transfer to a demijohn and fit an air lock, ferment to dryness. This wine takes about six months to a year to be at its best.

MODERN ELDERFLOWER WINE

This is more expensive, but the quality of the wine, which is probably unsurpassed in white country wines, certainly warrants the extra cost.

6 elderflower heads
1 can grape juice concentrate
15 oz (0.5 kg) can of gooseberries
yeast

Prepare the elderflowers as described in the previous recipes, cover with two pints (1 litre) of boiling water, and allow to cool. Add the gooseberries, with syrup, add the grape juice concentrate, taking care to wash the last remaining traces from the can with a little warm, but not boiling water. Adjust the volume to seven pints (4 litres). Add the yeast at 70°F (21°C). After one week, strain the liquid, gently squeezing the fruit, transfer to a demijohn, fit an air lock and ferment to dryness. The wine is ready for drinking when it has cleared, which is usually after three months.

See also Sultana, banana and elderflower wine (November) and Tea wine (March).

ROSE PETAL WINE

Rose petal wine is a bonus, the petals are collected after the blooms have blown and would normally be cut from the plant and discarded. Gather the heads and remove the petals which alone are used for winemaking. With rose petal wine the final bouquet is the same as that of the flowers themselves, so by making one gallon (4.5 litres) or two (9 litres) of the wine you can have 'June in January'. Since the finished wine will vary a great deal with the fragrance of the variety used, the quantity of petals must be adjusted accordingly. Use four pints (2 litres) of a mild scented rose or two pints (1 litre) of a strongly perfumed variety. Many authorities advocate using only one type of rose petal but this is seldom practical for most people with a small garden. You may mix them, the only disadvantage is that you will not necessarily be able to make the identical wine again, but that's all part of the fun.

2 to 4 pints (1 to 2 litres) rose petals (depending on variety)
1 lb (0.5 kg) sultanas
2½ lb (1.25 kg) sugar
2 tsp citric acid
pectic enzyme
yeast

Remove the petals, place in a bucket and make the wine according to the method given for traditional country elderflower.

Do not expect your rose petal wine to be rose in colour, this only occurs with salmon pink blooms and then not always.

CLARY WINE

This is a traditional wine which was made from clary flowers.

This plant which is closely related to the garden sage is now almost extinct in this country, although it is still fairly common around the Mediterranean.

To make the wine, take one pint (0.5 litre) of flowers and make by the method described for dandelion wine.

HERB WINES

A wide variety of herbs have been used for winemaking but, with the exception of parsley, these are generally not worth making. Indeed the flavour of parsley wine is so similar to elderflowers that it is not advisable to make both types of wine, but initially you may try to see which you prefer.

PARSLEY WINE

12 sprigs of parsley
1 lb (0.5 kg) sultanas
2 lb (1 kg) sugar
2 oranges
1 lemon
pectic enzyme
yeast

Use only freshly picked parsley, pour four pints (2 litres) of boiling water on to the parsley and the minced sultanas. Stir in the sugar until dissolved and add the juice of the oranges and lemon, ensuring that none of the white pith is allowed to enter the must. When the temperature has dropped to 70°F (21°C) add both the yeast and the pectic enzyme. Strain after four days, transfer to a demijohn and top up with water. Fit an air lock and ferment to dryness. This wine is ready for drinking as a light luncheon wine after about four months.

LETTUCE WINE

The so called lettuce wine is really only a sultana or raisin wine and the lettuce contributes nothing, not even flavour. If, however, you wish to make this wine, replace the parsley in the previous recipe with two (chopped up) medium sized lettuce.

OAK LEAF WINE

Oak leaves provide mainly tannin which allows you to make an acceptable wine at very low cost. Pick only the young leaves that have just started to grow.

6 pints (3 litres) young oak leaves
3 lb (1.5 kg) sugar
1½ lb (0.75 kg) bananas
2 oranges
1 lemon
yeast

Make sure that the leaves are free from any pieces of twig. Wash thoroughly and place in a bucket with four pints (2 litres) of boiling water and cover the bucket. When cool enough to handle stir in the sugar and the juice from the oranges and lemon. When tepid add the yeast. Stir. After twenty four hours (forty eight if you did not use a yeast starter) strain the liquid into a demijohn and make the volume up to about six pints (3 litres). After a week add the juice obtained from simmering the peeled bananas in a pint (0.5 litre) of water for twenty minutes. If any space remains top up the container with tap water.

You may omit the bananas if you wish, but the finished wine tends to be rather thin.

LOGANBERRY OR RASPBERRY WINE

Both of these fruits provide an excellent flavour to wines, but if used on their own, in sufficient quantities to give the wine enough body, tend to be far too acid. For this reason it is better to cut down on the fruit and incorporate sultanas in the recipe. These wines cannot be fermented on the must as the pips tend to give the wine an off flavour. If you have a juice extractor then simply extract the juice, bring to the boil with four pints (2 litres) of water, and use for wine making. If you do not possess the necessary equipment then follow the recommended method.

> 3 lb (1.5 kg) loganberries
> or 4 lb (2 kg) raspberries
> ½ lb (0.5 kg) sultanas
> 2½ lb (1.25 kg) sugar
> pectic enzyme
> yeast

Cover the mashed fruit and minced sultanas with boiling water in a bucket. When cool enough to handle, strain the liquid into a second bucket. Return the fruit to the first bucket and cover again with boiling water. Strain again into the other bucket, this time gently squeezing the pulp, which should be discarded after this operation. Dissolve the sugar in two pints (1 litre) of water and add to the liquid. If you have more than six pints (3 litres) of liquid from the juicing process add the sugar as a solid and stir to dissolve, but this is a more laborious task. Allow the temperature to reach 70°F (21°C), add the yeast and pectic enzyme. As no straining is involved the must can be transferred to the demijohn as soon as the initial fermentation has ceased. This makes a very dry light wine.

STRAWBERRY WINE

Providing you use only sound fruit, taking great care to remove any decayed or 'soft' berries, strawberries can be used to make a fine delicate wine.

> 3 lb (1.5 kg) strawberries
> 3 lb (1.5 kg) sugar
> 2 tsp citric acid
> yeast

Place the sugar and washed strawberries in a bucket and cover with five pints (3 litres) of boiling water. Stir thoroughly to dissolve the sugar, at the same time mashing the strawberries. When the liquid has dropped to the fermentation temperature add the yeast.

With strawberries there is no need to use pectic enzyme. After one week, strain, transfer to a demijohn and ferment to dryness.

This will produce a medium dry wine, sweeten to taste prior to serving rather than incorporate extra sugar in the recipe, as there is insufficient acid and body to carry the extra alcohol that may result from the treatment.

Variations
1. The inclusion of half a pound (250 gm) of sultanas together with the strawberries results in a wine with a fuller body.
2. Replace two pints (1 litre) of boiling water, with the liquid obtained by simmering a pound (500 gm) of ripe bananas with a pint and a half (0.75 litre) of water. This also produces a fuller wine than is obtained from the standard recipe.

CHERRY WINE

*4 lb (2 kg) cherries
1 lb (0.5 kg) sultanas
2½ lb (1.25 kg) sugar
pectic enzyme
yeast*

As there is insufficient juice in the cherries to extract it is necessary to carry out part of the fermentation in the presence of the fruit. Unfortunately the alcohol formed during the fermentation dissolves substances from the wood and gives an unpleasant flavour to the wine. This problem can be overcome by removing the seeds before using the fruit. Place the fruit, sugar and minced sultanas in a bucket and cover with boiling water. Allow to stand for half an hour and make up to six pints (3 litres). At 70°F (21°C) add pectic enzyme and yeast. Strain the liquid after a fortnight. Place in a demijohn and make up to a gallon (4.5 litres). Fit an air lock and keep at 70°F (21°C) until fermentation is complete.

This will give you a medium sweet wine. If you want it dry, use only 2lb (1 kg) of sugar, the wine will still remain balanced. If you use morello cherries use only 3 lb (1.5 kg) of the fruit.
NOTE: When using very small fruit it is virtually impossible to remove all of the stones. Quality wines can be made from such fruits providing that you strain the liquid into another bucket once the stones have separated. Squeeze the solid mass to ensure the maximum of the flavourings is extracted. When employing this method it is preferable to use a pint (0.5 litre) of either red or white, depending upon the colour of the cherries, grape juice (instead of the sultanas), as an efficient extraction of sultanas may not occur during the period that it takes for the stones to separate from the fruits.

Do not use raisins to make cherry wine.

BLACKCURRANT WINE

This fruit is so full of flavour that only one pound (0.5 kg) is needed to give a delightful wine.

1 lb (0.5 kg) blackcurrants
1 lb (0.5 kg) sultanas
2½ lb (1.25 kg) sugar
1 tsp citric acid
pectic enzyme
yeast

Remove any tails from the fruit as these will impart a bitter taste. The dead brown tips will not affect the wine. Put the fruit in a bucket and crush thoroughly with a fork (if you possess a liquidiser it will extract the juice more efficiently, and the juiced fruit may be used instead), add the minced sultanas, the sugar, citric acid and cover with six pints (3 litres) of boiling water. Stir until all the sugar has dissolved. When the temperature is at 70°F (21°C) add the pectic enzyme and yeast. Allow the must to ferment for ten days, after which time it should be strained, transferred to a demijohn and an air lock fitted. If you wish to taste the full blackcurrant flavour drink whilst still fairly young. Sugar to taste may be added to the finished wine, without upsetting the balance.

ROSE PETAL ROSÉ

½ lb (250 gm) blackcurrants
½ lb (250 gm) sultanas
2 to 4 pints (1 to 2 litres) of rose petals (depending upon variety)
2½ lb (1.25 kg) sugar
2 tsp citric acid
pectic enzyme
yeast

Depending upon the intensity of perfume in the flowers, use either two or four pints (1 or 2 litres). You do not require any particular colour as the rosé shade and flavour will be provided by the blackcurrants. Check the petals to ensure that there is no dirt or insects present, remove any stalks from the blackcurrants. Place the petals, the crushed blackcurrants and sultanas and sugar in the bucket. Add half a gallon (2 litres) of boiling water, leave to cool slightly before stirring until all of the sugar has dissolved. Add two pints (1 litre) of cold water. At the fermentation temperature provide the citric acid, pectic enzyme and yeast. Strain when the vigorous head has subsided and finish in the usual manner. The wine is at its best when it is a year old.

RASPBERRY DESSERT

As an alternative to the medium dry raspberry wine it is possible to make a full bodied dessert.

4 lb (2 kg) raspberries
2 lb (1 kg) bananas
3 lb (1.5 kg) sugar
pectic enzyme
wine yeast

Prepare the raspberries as described in loganberry or raspberry wine. Prepare an extract of the bananas by simmering the peeled fruit in two pints (1 litre) of water for twenty minutes. Place in a bucket with two and a half pounds (1.25 kgs) of sugar, stir until the solid has dissolved, then add sufficient tap water to make the total volume up to one gallon (4.5 litres). At 70°F (21°C) add the wine yeast and pectic enzyme. Transfer to a demijohn, when the vigorous fermentation is complete, straining should not be necessary. Ferment to dryness, racking as necessary, then feed with two four ounce (110 gm) portions of sugar to produce a sweet high alcohol wine. As with all dessert wines this particular style requires two years to reach perfection and it will keep for many years beyond this time.

Variation
Replace one pound (0.5 kg) of bananas with the same quantity of sultanas. Add the sultanas to the raspberries.

BURNET WINE

3 pints (1.5 litres) burnet leaves (loose packed)
1 lb (0.5 kg) sultanas
2½ lb (1.25 kg) sugar
2 tsp citric acid
yeast

This is an example of an old fashioned country wine with the method changed to afford a more modern and acceptable drink. Gather three pints (1.5 litres) of salad burnet leaves, place in a muslin bag and bring to the boil in four pints (2 litres) of water. Simmer for thirty minutes. Pour the liquid on to the sugar and chopped sultanas. Dissolve the sugar before making up to a gallon (4.5 litres) (this will require a further 2½–3½ pints (1.25–1.75 litres). At 70°F (21°C) add the yeast and stir daily. When the initial fermentation has ceased strain the wine into a demijohn and finish in the usual manner. Keep for six months to a year.

OTHER WINES TO MAKE DURING JUNE

Dried sloe and banana (see January)
Grapefruit, prune, gooseberry, bilberry, pineapple and lychees, mixed fruit, raisin and banana (see February)
Tea, cranberry, dried elderberry, dried orange blossom, dried peach, fig and banana, dried sloe (see March)
Grapefruit, orange, dried rosehip and banana (see April)
Ginger, banana, rhubarb and elderflower (see May)
Gooseberry, loganberry, raspberry, pea pod, rhubarb champagne, dried apricot and banana, date and banana (see July)
Rice, dried prune, dried date, dried apricot (see November)
Sultanas, bananas and elderflower (see December)

JULY

The two most important ingredients for winemaking in July are soft fruit and honey. If you possess a greenhouse and the temperature is not allowed to rise above 75°F (21°C) you can allow your wine to ferment under the staging providing that you cover the demijohn with paper to stop direct sunlight turning the wines brown.

MEAD

Unless you are a beekeeper mead is the most expensive of all wines to make, nevertheless it can be so good that it is well worth the extra cost. When making mead use only light honeys. Do not under any circumstances make it from the heavily scented honeys, such as eucalyptus. Many beekeepers take their honey during the last week in July and if you can buy some unripe honey it is ideal, and often cheap.

SWEET MEAD

---

4 lb (2 kg) honey
2½ tsp citic acid
nutrient
yeast

Honey is deficient in many nutrients found in fruit and consequently it is absolutely essential to employ a good yeast nutrient. One method used to provide vitamin B1, one of the deficient minerals, was to add Marmite but as yeast requires other additives to ferment out it is best to add a balanced wine nutrient.

Due to the problems of fermentation, you must also use a yeast starter. Into a sterilised milk bottle place three ounces (75 gm) of sugar, the tip of a teaspoon of citric acid and half a pint (250 ml) of water and the yeast. Place cling film over the top of the bottle and place in a fermentation cabinet or other warm place. The yeast starter is ready for adding to the must when the mixture is working vigorously, which is usually after forty eight hours. Place the honey in a sterilised bucket, and add four pints (2 litres) of boiling water — like with flower wines some authorities advocate never adding boiling water to honey, but because of the dangers of wild yeast it is essential to completely sterilise the honey. Allow the temperature to drop to 70°F (21°C) – 65°F (18°C) if you are using a mead yeast starter which is not essential, add the acid nutrient and active yeast starter. Transfer to a demijohn. Top up after one week if an air space remains.

Mead is far slower maturing than other wines and preferably should not be drunk until it is at least two years old.

POOR MAN'S MEAD I

1½ lb (0.75 kg) honey
1 lb (0.5 kg) sultanas
1½ lb (0.75 kg) sugar
2 tsp citric acid
nutrient
yeast

Do not mince the sultanas, as clearing problems may develop with this particular type of wine.

Place the honey, sultanas and sugar in a bucket, add four pints (2 litres) of boiling water. Allow to cool to 70°F (21°C), add the yeast and nutrient. Strain after ten days, transfer to a demijohn, top up and ferment to dryness.

POOR MAN'S MEAD II

2 lb (1 kg) honey
1 lb (0.5 kg) bananas
1 lb (0.5 kg) sugar
2 tsp citric acid
nutrient
yeast

Discard the peel from the bananas and simmer the fruit for twenty minutes in two pints (1 litre) of water. Strain and lightly squeeze, pour on to the sugar and honey, together with four pints (2 litres) of boiling water.

When cool transfer to a demijohn and add citric acid, nutrient and yeast. After twelve days fill up the jar with tap water, ferment to dryness and bottle.

DRY MEAD

This may be made according to the method given for sweet mead but three pounds (1.5 kg) instead of four pounds (2 kg) of honey should be employed.

PEA POD WINE

This wine is a bonus as pea pods are usually thrown on the compost heap. They do form the basis of a good wine as they give almost as much body weight for weight as raisins. However, they do lack flavour, sugar and tannin. For this reason it is usual to include half a pound (250 gm) of raisins in the wine. Alternatively you may use the pea pods as the basis of your flower wine. Use a half pound (250 gm) with quantities of flowers given under the appropriate recipes, but omit the sultanas. See pea pod and elderflower wine.

2 lb (1 kg) pea pods
2½ lb (1.25 kg) sugar
½ lb (250 gm) raisins
2 lemons
1 orange
pectic enzyme
yeast

Pour six pints (3 litres) of boiling water on to the pea pods and raisins, then stir in the sugar until dissolved. Squeeze the juice of the orange and lemons into the must allowing none of the white pith to enter. Allow the temperature to drop to 70°F (21°C) then add the yeast and pectic enzyme. Stir the mixture daily. When the initial head has subsided, strain the wine into a demijohn and ferment until bubbles cease to escape from the air lock. Rack and bottle. This is a medium sweet wine.

PEA POD AND ELDERFLOWER

The pea and elderflower season overlap and the two ingredients may be used economically together.

1 lb (0.5 kg) pea pods
12 elderflower heads
2½ lb (1.25 kg) sugar
2 tsp citric acid (or 2 lemons)
12 drops grape juice tannin
or 1 cup medium strength tea (without milk)
yeast

One of the cheapest of all wines. It has the advantage that it can be made entirely without the addition of chemicals.

Two days before they are required, place the elderflowers in a plastic bag and put into the freezer compartment of your refrigerator. Take out the bag, shake well to dislodge all the petals, these will separate easily. Discard the stalks and transfer the petals to a bucket. Add all the other ingredients, except the yeast, and pour on six pints (3 litres) of boiling water. Allow to cool, then add the yeast. After a week transfer to a demijohn, top up and fit an air lock. Ferment to dryness, at which stage the wine is immediately ready for drinking.

HONEYSUCKLE WINE

Honeysuckle berries are poisonous, and under no circumstances should they be used for winemaking. But the flowers can be used to give a wine with a delightful bouquet.

2 pints (1 litre) honeysuckle flowers
1 lb (0.5 kg) sultanas
2½ lb (1.25 kg) sugar
2 tsp citric acid
pectic enzyme
yeast

Pick only fully opened flowers of the wild variety. Strip away any remaining green material and place in a bucket together with the sugar, minced sultanas and citric acid. Add six pints (3 litre) of boiling water and stir thoroughly. Add the pectic enzyme and yeast at 65–70°F (18–21°C) and cover. Stir daily for four days then strain into a demijohn. If necessary top up, and then fit an air lock. Fermentation may take up to three months when the medium sweet wine should be bottled. It may be drunk immediately, but like all sweet wines will improve with keeping.

LIME PETAL WINE

This is another old recipe, it requires the flowers of the lime tree. For all lime wines use one pint (0.5 litre) of flowers.

1 pint (0.5 litre) lime flowers
1 lb (0.5 kg) sultanas
2½ lb (1.25 kg) sugar
2 tsp citric acid
pectic enzyme
yeast

Into a fermenting bucket place the flowers and sultanas, cover with three pints (1.5 litres) of boiling water, stir in the sugar until it dissolves. Make up to one gallon (4.5 litres) with tap water. Add the acid, yeast and pectic enzyme at about 70°F (21°C). Stir daily. Strain after seven days — do not delay as the lime petals will begin to decompose. Transfer to a demijohn, fit an air lock. Ferment to a medium dry wine which can be sweetened by the addition of extra sugar.
    The wine may be drunk after nine months.

Variation
Replace the sultanas with 20 fl oz (0.5 litre) of white grape juice. The grape juice should be added after the petals have been scalded. Reduce the volume of water to allow for the grape juice.

RHUBARB CHAMPAGNE

3 lb (1.5 kg) rhubarb
2½ lb (1.25 kg) sugar
champagne or general wine yeast

Cut the rhubarb into pieces about two inches (5 cm) in length (do not peel) and place in a fermenting bucket with a tight fitting lid. Leave for one month. Remove all of the scum that develops, then strain into another bucket, squeezing the remains of the rhubarb gently. Add the sugar and yeast. Stir and leave in the bucket for a further week. Transfer to a demijohn, top up, fit an air lock and ferment to dryness. Transfer to a champagne or any sparkling wine bottle weighing approximately 900 gm. Add a level teaspoonful of sugar, fit a cork and wire down as described on page 31 and stand in a warm place for three weeks. The wine may be drunk after a further six weeks and will keep for several years. Before serving allow the wine to stand in the refrigerator for four hours.

GOOSEBERRY WINE

Gooseberry is one of the finest ingredients for winemaking.

4 lb (2 kg) gooseberries
3½ lb (1.75 kg) sugar
12 drops grape juice tannin
or 1 cup of tea (without milk)
pectic enzyme
yeast

Cover the fruit with water in a saucepan and bring to the boil, taking care not to overheat which will caramelise the natural sugars. Cool, transfer to a bucket and mash the fruit. Dissolve the sugar in two pints of water and add this together with the tannin or cold tea. Add one pint (0.5 litre) of cold water and allow to cool to 70°F (21°C). At this stage add the yeast and pectic enzyme. After a week, but no longer, strain, transfer to a demijohn and ferment in the usual way.

GOOSEBERRY AND ELDERFLOWER WINE

Home preserve makers have known for years that the addition of a handful of elderflowers greatly adds to the attractions of gooseberry jam. The flowers have an equally beneficial effect on wine, a small quantity giving a subtle flowery bouquet to one of our finest country wines.

3 lb (1.5 kg) gooseberries
½ lb (250 gm) sultanas
2¾ lb (1.4 kg) sugar
4 heads of elderflowers
pectic enzyme
yeast

Place the gooseberries in a bucket and crush with a potato masher. Add the sultanas and the petals of the elderflowers in a muslin bag. Cover with two pints (1 litre) of hot water before adding to the other ingredients. Provide a further two pints (1 litre) of cold water. At 65–70°F (18.5–21°C) add the yeast and pectic enzyme. Remove the bag after 72 hours. After seven to ten days, strain, transfer to a demijohn, top up if necessary and ferment to dryness. Drink as soon as the wine is clear.

Read general notes on elderflower wines on page 79.

GOOSEBERRY AND BLACKCURRANT WINE

2 lb (1 kg) gooseberries
2 lb (1 kg) blackcurrants
1 lb (0.5 kg) sultanas or raisins
2¾ lb (1.4 kg) sugar
pectic enzyme
yeast

Remove the stalks from the fruit, place in the bucket and crush with a potato masher or break up with a fork. Add the sultanas or raisins together with four pints (2 litres) of boiling water. Stir in the sugar, before adding one and a half pints (0.75 litre) of cold water. At about 70°F (21°C) provide both the pectic enzyme and yeast. Stir daily. When the initial fermentation has subsided, usually after seven to ten days, strain, very gently squeezing the solids before transferring to a demijohn and top up if necessary. Rack this medium sweet wine as required. Do not drink until it is at least nine months old.

OTHER WINES TO MAKE DURING JULY

Dried sloe and banana (see January)
Grapefruit, prune, bilberry, pineapple and lychees, mixed fruit, raisin and banana (see February)
Tea, cranberry, dried elderberry, dried orange blossom, dried peach, fig and banana, dried sloe (see March)
Grapefruit, orange, dried rosehip and banana (see April)
Ginger, banana, rhubarb and elderflower (see May)
Rose petal, parsley, elderflower (see June)
White currant (see August)
Rice, raisin, dried prune, dried apricot, dried date, dried apricot and banana, date and banana (see November)
Sultana, banana and elderflower (see December)

W·I·N·E·M·A·K·I·N·G M·O·N·T·H B·Y M·O·N·T·H
AUGUST

There is an increasing abundance of home grown fruit and imported fruit at their cheapest at this time of year.

RED CURRANT WINE

Red currants are best employed to make a rosé wine. To develop the depth of colour it is necessary to ferment on the fruit rather than extract the juices first.

3½ lb (1.75 kg) red currants
2½ lb (1.25 kg) sugar
pectic enzyme
wine yeast

Remove the stalks from the fruit, and wash to ensure that there is no dirt on the berries, then place in a fermentation bucket. Crush the fruit with a potato masher, add four pints (2 litres) of boiling water and stir in the sugar until dissolved. When cool make up to a gallon (4.5 litres) with tap water. At 70°F (21°C) add the pectic enzyme and the wine yeast. Stir daily. If you prefer a light rosé coloured wine strain the liquid after three days into a second fermenting bucket and allow to remain there for a further four days. For a deeper rosé conduct the initial ferment entirely in the presence of the fruit and strain after seven days. In either case the liquid should be fermented under an air lock a week after the wine was started.

Rosé wines are particularly susceptible to oxidation and unless care is taken the liquid quickly acquires a brown hue and the delicate flavour is similarly affected. Overcome the problem by ensuring that the fermentation is conducted in the dark and that the wine is stored in brown or green bottles. Add a Campden tablet to each gallon (4.5 litres) of wine after fermentation is complete. Even with these precautions the wine which is ready after four months is best drunk before it is eighteen months old.

WHITE CURRANT WINE

This is one of the best dessert wines, being quick maturing and possessing good keeping qualities.

3 lb (1.5 kg) white currants
3½ lb (1.75 kg) sugar
glycerine
yeast

Remove the tails from the fruit and place in a bucket with three pounds (1.5 kg) of the sugar and cover with five pints (2.5 litres) of boiling water. When cool, stir until all of the sugar has dissolved and at 70°F (21°C) add the yeast. Stir daily, mashing the fruit against the wall of the bucket with a wooden spoon. After ten days strain the must through muslin, but do not squeeze. Transfer to a demijohn, and add a further half pound (250 gm) of sugar dissolved in a small quantity of water. Fit an air lock and ferment until the wine stops working. The addition of glycerine at the rate of one teaspoonful per bottle greatly improves the quality of the finished wine.

GREENGAGE WINE

4 lb (2 kg) greegages
3 lb (1.5 kg) sugar
yeast

Remove the stones from the greengages and place together with the sugar in a fermenting bucket fitted with a lid. Add five pints (2.5 litres) of boiling water. Stir until the sugar has dissolved, and when cool add the yeast. Strain after five days, transfer to a demijohn, top up with water and ferment to dryness.

This is a delicate wine which will quickly darken if allowed to come into contact with the air.

For a fuller greengage wine, make according to the method given for plums (September) replacing the plums with an equal quantity of greengages.

DAMSON WINE

Damsons are high in both acid and tannin and consequently only a small quantity is needed. To make a good damson wine requires a little more effort than most wines, but it is the only way to make a really good drink.

2 lb (1.0 kg) damsons
1 lb (0.5 kg) sultanas
3 lb (1.5 kg) sugar
pectic enzyme
yeast

Cover the sugar and the damsons with five pints (2.5 litres) of boiling water. When cool stir to dissolve the sugar, add both the yeast and pectic enzyme. Cover and allow to ferment for three days — but no longer. Strain into a second bucket containing the sultanas — these should not be minced — and make up to one gallon (4.5 litres). Leave in the bucket for a fortnight stirring daily. Then strain, transfer to a demijohn and ferment to dryness. This wine should be medium sweet and glycerine may be added at the rate of one teaspoonful per bottle to the finished wine at the time of bottling. Leave to mature in the bottle for a year.

BEETROOT WINE

Beetroot wine can be made at any time between August and October, but since there is so much wine to make during the next two months, it is advisable to make this wine as early as possible.

4 lb (2 kg) beetroot
3½ lb (1.75 kg) sugar
¼ oz (7 gm) ginger (optional)
2 tsp citric acid
yeast

Wash well, but do not peel the beetroot, dice and bring to the boil in about six pints (3 litres) of water. Simmer for half an hour, strain, reject the solid and pour the liquid on to 3 lb (1.75 kg) of sugar, in a bucket. Stir until the sugar has dissolved, then add the citric acid and the ginger. Ginger has a most pronounced effect on the flavour of the wine and it is solely a matter of personal choice whether or not you include it. Allow to cool, transfer to a demijohn, add no further water at this stage but do add the yeast. Fit an air lock. After one week, top up the container with water and replace the air lock. When the first heavy sediment forms rack the wine, even though fermentation is not complete. Dissolve a further half pound (250 gm) of the sugar in a quarter of a pint (125 ml) of water and use this to top up the liquid after racking. Replace the air lock. After fermentation there should be a slight, but not excessive residual sweetness. If the wine is still dry, which occasionally happens, rack, add a quarter pound (125 gm) of sugar dissolved in the minimum amount of water and one Campden tablet. Store away from light, otherwise the wine rapidly develops a tawny colour.

PEACH WINE

Bruised and damaged peaches can be obtained from greengrocers and markets very cheaply at this time of the year. Peaches, unfortunately, provide very little body and it is necessary to add a second ingredient. If you use bananas the wine will retain its golden colour and the two flavours marry together to give a superb wine.

> 3 lb (1.5 kg) peaches
> 1 lb (0.5 kg) bananas
> 3 lb (1.5 kg) sugar
> ½ tsp citric acid
> pectic enzyme
> yeast

Simmer the peeled bananas in a pint (0.5 litre) of boiling water for twenty minutes, then strain but do not squeeze.

Remove the stones from the peaches, place in a bucket and cover with four pints (2 litres) of boiling water. When cool add the banana juice, sugar, pectic enzyme and yeast. Stir until the sugar is dissolved. Leave for two or three days, strain and transfer to a demijohn. Do not top up at this stage, wait until the initial fermentation has died down. Ferment to dryness.

Variations
Whilst it is possible to make a peach wine by replacing the bananas with an equal weight of sultanas, there is a danger that the character of the dried fruit will predominate at the expense of the peaches. This is overcome by the addition of a pint (0.5 litre) of pure grape juice.

Never add flowers to a peach wine as the two bouquets and flavours do not blend.

GRAPE PRUNINGS WINE

At this time of the year grapes should have a light pruning and unlike most green materials, these prunings can be used to make a most acceptable wine. Since most of the materials that will go to make the grape will travel up the stems, it is not surprising that such a good wine results.

> 1 gallon (4.5 litres) lightly pressed vine leaves and soft wood prunings
> 3 lb (1.5 kg) sugar
> 1½ tsp citric acid
> yeast

Wash the prunings and make sure that they are free from insects.

To the prunings, which should measure one gallon (4.5 litres) when lightly pressed, add six pints (3 litres) of boiling water and cover the bucket. Leave standing with frequent stirring for three days. Strain the liquid into another bucket containing the sugar and citric acid. Add the yeast and allow to ferment until the vigorous head has subsided, this usually takes a week to ten days. Transfer to a demijohn, top up, fit an air lock and ferment to dryness.

GRAPE AND RAISIN WINE

During August fresh grapes, especially the sultana type which are ideal for our purpose, can usually be bought fairly cheaply. Whilst it would be too expensive to buy enough grapes to make the wine solely from this ingredient a very good aperitif can be made from a mixture of grapes and raisins.

1½ lb (0.75 kg) grapes
½ lb (225 gm) brown sugar
1 lb (0.5 kg) raisins
2½ lb (1.25 kg) white sugar
yeast

Crush the grapes in the fermenting bucket and add the minced raisins together with four pints (2 litres) of boiling water. Add the sugar, dissolved in two pints (1 litre) of water, with constant stirring. Allow the must to cool and add the yeast. Strain after a fortnight and transfer to a demijohn. Top up, fit an air lock and ferment until the wine ceases to work.

This wine is not really ready for drinking for a year and goes on improving for another two years.

It is a sweet wine with a sherry type flavour.

APPLE AND DAMSON WINE

This is a light rosé table wine.

3 lb (1.5 kg) apples
¾ lb (350 gm) damsons
2¾ lb (1.4 kg) sugar
pectic enzyme
yeast

To maintain the delicate colour it is necessary to use Campden tablets, which in turn requires the production of a yeast starter.

Wash the apples and remove the decayed parts of the fruit, but do not peel. Cut the damsons in half, before adding to the apples in the bucket. Add four pints (2 litres) of cold water, sugar and a Campden tablet. Cover and allow to stand for twenty-four hours, then add a vigorous working starter. As soon as the stones separate, remove with a spoon. After seven days strain, gently squeeze and transfer to a demijohn, top up if necessary and ferment to dryness. Rack and add one Campden tablet per gallon (4.5 litres).

This particular brew is ideal as a semi-sparkling wine. To prepare this drink omit the Campden tablet at the racking stage. Bottle in champagne bottles, adding half a teaspoonful of sugar to each bottle. Cork and wire down as described under sparkling wine, then stand at fermentation temperature for a fortnight. With either style wine it is ready for drinking one month after racking.

TROPICAL FRUIT WINE

1 lb (0.5 kg) apricots
1 lb (0.5 kg) peaches
1 lb (0.5 kg) bananas
1 lb (0.5 kg) sultanas
2¾ lb (1.4 kg) sugar
1 orange
1 lemon
pectic enzyme
yeast

Stone the apricots and peaches before placing them in the fermentation bucket. Add the sultanas and the juice of the orange and lemon, cover with two pints (1 litre) of boiling water. Extract the bananas by simmering the fruit with one and a half pints (0.75 litre) of water for twenty minutes. Strain the liquid into the bucket, discarding the pulp. Add two and a quarter pounds (1.1 kg) of the sugar and stir until dissolved. Make up to one gallon (4.5 litres) and at 70°F (21°C) add the yeast and pectic enzyme. Strain after seven to ten days. Continue the fermentation under air lock. When fermentation is complete, rack, feed with four ounces (110 gm) of sugar and ferment until evolution of bubbles ceases. If the wine is still dry repeat the feeding procedure. The wine is best kept for a year and will last for several years without showing signs of decay.

APRICOT WINE

Unlike many wines, apricot retains the delicate fruit flavour. Like peaches, it is often possible to buy bruised apricots. Provided that the decayed fruit has been cut out, these are suitable for winemaking.

4 lb (2 kg) apricots
1 lb (0.5 kg) sultanas
2½ lb (1.25 kg) sugar
pectic enzyme
yeast

Stone the fruit, mince the sultanas and place together with the sugar in a bucket. Cover with four pints (2 litres) of boiling water and stir until all the sugar has dissolved. Add a further two pints (1 litre) of cold water and when the temperature has dropped to 70°F (21°C) add the yeast and pectic enzyme. Allow to ferment for one week then strain, without squeezing.

Transfer to a demijohn, fit an air lock and ferment to dryness. Sultanas give a light brown colour to the wine.

If you prefer a lighter coloured wine replace the sultanas with an extra half pound (250 gm) of sugar. This wine lacks the body of that made by the standard recipe, but it is still delicious, with slightly more of the apricot character coming through.

Variations
The sultanas may be replaced with a pound (0.5 kilo) of bananas and half a teaspoon of citric acid and the wine made according to the method given for peach wine.

Alternatively, the sultanas may be replaced by a pint of white grape juice and the total volume adjusted accordingly.

OTHER WINES TO MAKE DURING AUGUST

Dried sloe and banana (see January)
Grapefruit, prune, gooseberry, bilberry, pineapple and lychees, raisin and banana, mixed fruit (see February)
Tea, cranberry, dried elderberry, dried orange blossom, dried peach, dried sloe, fig and banana (see March)
Orange, grapefruit, dried rosehip and banana (see April)
Ginger, banana (see May)
Elderflower, rose petal (see June)
Honeysuckle, pea pod, blackcurrant, mead (see July)
Plum, blackberry (see September)

Rice, raisin, dried prune, dried apricot, dried date, dried apricot and banana, date and banana (see November)
Sultana, banana and elderflower (see December)

W·I·N·E·M·A·K·I·N·G M·O·N·T·H B·Y M·O·N·T·H
SEPTEMBER

September is the busiest of all months in the winemaker's calendar. During this month virtually all the fruit for making red wines should be collected (with the possible exception of sloe). Fruit not needed immediately for winemaking should be frozen for use later in the year.

BLACKBERRY WINE

Providing the juice is carefully extracted blackberries produce the finest of all country wines.

When picking blackberries, try to gather the fruit as far away from the main road as possible, to avoid contamination by lead from exhaust pipes and diesel fumes which give an off flavour to the wine.

EXTRACTION OF JUICE

Place the fruit in a bucket and cover with boiling water. Cover the bucket with a suitable air-tight lid. Allow to stand until cool enough to handle, strain the juice through muslin into a second bucket. Return the fruit to the first bucket and again cover with boiling water. Repeat the straining through the muslin, this time gently squeezing the fruit ensuring that no pips, which would give the wine a woody taste, are allowed to pass through into the juice.

BLACKBERRY PORT

This is a full bodied red dessert wine.

4 lb (2 kg) blackberries
1 lb (0.5 kg) raisins
1 lb (0.5 kg) bananas
3 lb (1.5 kg) sugar
pectic enzyme
yeast

Extract the blackberry juice according to the method given above. Prepare the banana juice by simmering the peeled bananas in two pints (1 litre) of water for twenty minutes and straining. Add these two liquids to the minced raisins, which had previously been covered with the minimum amount of boiling water in a bucket. Dissolve two pounds (1 kg) of the sugar in a pint (0.75 litre) of water and include this in the must. If necessary adjust the total volume to between six and seven pints (4 litres). Add the yeast and the pectic enzyme. Strain after ten days and add a further half pound (250 gm) of sugar dissolved in half a pint (250 ml) water, transfer to a demijohn, top up and fit an air lock. Rack after the first heavy sediment has formed and again top up with a further half pound (250 gm) of sugar and sufficient water to refill the jar, refit air lock and ferment until no further bubbles are seen to escape. The wine may be drunk as it is, but it can be improved by the addition of a tablespoonful of glycerine per bottle. The further addition of either the same quantity of vodka, better still brandy, promotes the wine almost to the liqueur class.

BLACKBERRY WINE

4 lb (2 kg) blackberries
3 lb (1.5 kg) sugar
pectic enzyme
yeast

This is a basic blackberry recipe that gives a very cheap, light dry table wine that may be sweetened to taste at the time of serving.

Prepare the blackberry juice according to the general method given. Dissolve the sugar in two pints (1 litre) of water. Transfer both the liquids to a demijohn, make the total volume up to seven pints (4 litres), provide both the yeast and the pectic enzyme; fit an air lock. After the vigorous fermentation has subsided fill the demijohn with water and refit the air lock. This wine is best drunk young, when it still retains its fresh fruity flavour.

MOCK CLARET

This wine is one of the best table wines that the amateur can hope to make.

1½ lb (0.75 kg) blackberries
1 tin red grape juice concentrate
¾ lb (0.5 kg) sugar
pectic enzyme
yeast

Juice the blackberries according to the method given above; dissolve the sugar in a pint (0.5 litre) of water and place straight into the demijohn together with the grape juice concentrate. Wash the remains of the concentrate from the can into the vessel ensuring that there is a two–three inch (5–7 cm) air space remaining. Add yeast and pectic enzyme when tepid, and fit an air lock. Ferment to dryness.

    This wine requires only a short fermentation and maturation period and will be ready to complement the turkey this Christmas.

BLACKBERRY AND SULTANA WINE

Blackberries are such a versatile ingredient, that they may be used to make every possible type of red wine.
    This recipe gives a medium sweet wine.

3 lb (1.5 kg) blackberries
1 lb (0.5 kg) sultanas
2½ lb (1.25 kg) sugar
pectic enzyme
yeast

Place the blackberries, minced sultanas and sugar in the bucket, add five pints (3 litres) of boiling water. Stir to dissolve the sugar. When the temperature has dropped to 70°F (21°C) add the yeast and pectic enzyme. After four days strain the liquid through muslin, gently squeeze the bag, and transfer to a demijohn. Top up with tap water, fit an air lock and rack when the wine becomes clear.

ELDERBERRIES

This is one of the most useful of all fruits to the home winemaker, but it is very high in tannin and unless care is taken in the extraction of the juice the wine may take several years to mature.

The recipes and methods given below yield wines which in many respects are similar to the style of commercial wines. However, some winemakers feel that they lack the unique irony or flinty character which was once the hallmark of an elderberry wine. If you wish to incorporate this character, without the problem of the excess maturation period and harshness of the traditional elderberry, add a handful of berries to the must. These must be sterilised by immersion in boiling water and removed by sieving immediately that the initial fermentation has ceased.

ELDERBERRY PORT

2 lb (1 kg) elderberries
1 lb (0.5 kg) raisins
1 lb (0.5 kg) bananas
3 lb (1.5 kg) sugar
2 tsp citric acid
pectic enzyme
yeast

Remove the fruit from the stems (the weights given refer to the berries after they have been stripped from the stems) and place in a bucket. Mash the fruit thoroughly with a fork and cover with two pints (1 litre) of boiling water. Allow to cool, strain through muslin and gently squeeze.

The wine should be made according to the method given for blackberry port, the citric acid being added at the same stage as the yeast.

ELDERBERRY WINE

This recipe produces a very cheap wine that does not require liquidising the fruit. It is ready for drinking after about a year.

2 lb (1 kg) elderberries
3 lb (1.5 kg) sugar
2 tsp citric acid
pectic enzyme
yeast

Cover the berries with four pints (2 litres) of boiling water, stir in the sugar and add the acid. Allow to cool to 70°F (21°C) at which temperature the yeast and pectic enzyme should be added. After forty eight hours — but no longer, as the newly formed alcohol will dissolve too much tannin out of the fruit — strain but do not squeeze the fruit. Transfer to a demijohn. After a further five days top up the demijohn with water and ferment to dryness.

ELDERBERRY BURGUNDY

1½ lb (0.75 kg) elderberries
1 tin red grape juice concentrate
¾ lb (0.5 kg) sugar
1 tsp citric acid
pectic enzyme
yeast

This wine should be made by the method given for blackberry claret, the citric acid being added at the same time as the yeast. This gives a robust wine. If you like burgundy you will love this wine.

BILBERRIES AND BLUEBERRIES

Bilberries and blueberries, which are very similar, make wines that are probably superior even to blackberry and elderberry wines, but unfortunately the fruit is often far more difficult to find.

BILBERRY OR BLUEBERRY PORT

3 lb (1.5 kg) bilberries or blueberries
1 lb (0.5 kg) raisins
1 lb (0.5 kg) bananas
3 lb (1.5 kg) sugar
1 tsp citric acid
pectic enzyme
yeast

This wine should be made according to the recipe for blackberry port; the citric acid being added at the same time as the yeast.

SWEET BILBERRY AND BLACKBERRY

2 lb (1 kg) bilberries
3 lb (1.5 kg) blackberries
½ lb (250 gm) sultanas
1 lb (0.5 kg) bananas
3¼ lb (1.6 kg) sugar
pectic enzyme
yeast

Prepare the bilberries and blackberries as described under the dry wine. Prepare an extract of the bananas by simmering the peeled fruit for twenty minutes. Scald the sultanas with a pint (0.5 litre) of boiling water. Add the fruit (but not the water as the total may exceed a gallon (4.5 litres) depending upon the volume of liquid obtained from the fruit). Dissolve two and three quarter pounds (1.4 kg) of sugar in the liquid, then make up to one gallon (4.5 litres). At 70°F (21°C) add the yeast and pectic enzyme. Stir daily. After seven days, strain. Transfer to a demijohn and fit an air lock. Rack as necessary. When the wine is dry feed with four ounce (110 gm) portions of sugar until a sweet maximum alcohol wine is obtained. Store for at least a year.

BILBERRY OR BLUEBERRY WINE

This gives a high alcohol, full bodied wine.

3 lb (1.5 kg) bilberries or blueberries
1 lb (0.5 kg) sultanas
2½ lb (1.25 kg) sugar
½ tsp citric acid
pectic enzyme
yeast

Wash the berries, place in a bucket together with the minced sultanas and mash thoroughly with a fork. Cover with four pints (2 litres) of boiling water and stir in the sugar until dissolved. Add a further two pints (1 litre) of tap water when the temperature has dropped to 70°F (21°C) add yeast, acid and pectic enzyme. Allow to ferment, stirring daily until the fruit is seen to float to the top (this usually occurs after about two days) but if it is still not observed after four days proceed to the next stage. Strain, do not squeeze, into a demijohn and fit an air lock. When the initial vigorous fermentation has subsided fill the jar with water. This wine which is medium sweet and may be further sweetened to taste, improves with keeping.

DRY BILBERRY AND BLACKBERRY WINE

2 lb (1 kg) bilberries
2 lb (1 kg) blackberries
2¾ lb (1.4 kg) sugar
pectic enzyme
yeast

Extract the blackberries, by first crushing and then covering with two pints (1 litre) of boiling water, strain into the fermenting bucket which should contain the crushed bilberries and a further pint (0.5 litre) of boiling water. Stir in and dissolve the sugar before making the total volume up to one gallon (4.5 litres). At the fermentation temperature add the yeast and pectic enzyme. Stir daily. As soon as the initial fermentation subsides, strain, transfer to a demijohn and fit an air lock. Allow to ferment to dryness. Rack and store in a dark bottle to retain the deep hue. Drink from one month after the wine has cleared.

BILBERRY OR BLUEBERRY CLARET

1½ lb (0.75 kg) bilberries or blueberries
1 tin red grape juice concentrate
¾ lb (350 gm) sugar
½ tsp citric acid
pectic enzyme
yeast

This wine should be made by the method given for blackberry claret, the citric acid being added at the same stage as the yeast.
This is a very fine red table wine.

MULBERRY WINE

Although scarce, if you are fortunate enough to acquire four pounds (2.0 kg) of mulberries they will make an excellent wine.

4 lb (2 kg) mulberries
1 lb (0.5 kg) sultanas
2½ lb (1.25 kg) sugar
pectic enzyme
yeast

Ideally the fruit should not be gathered until it has fallen from the tree, at which stage it will contain the maximum amount of sugar and the minimum of acid.

Mash the fruit in the bucket and cover with two pints (1 litre) of boiling water. Allow to stand for one hour. Strain, discard the pulp and pour the juice on to the sugar. Add a further four pints (2 litres) of tepid water, and stir until the sugar has dissolved. Add the yeast and pectic enzyme. After one week strain the liquid and transfer to a demijohn, ferment to dryness. This wine may be sweetened to taste.

APPLE WINE

A very cheap, light dry wine, which is excellent, can be made from apples. The exact flavour will depend upon the variety of apples used and how ripe they are.

Do not be tempted to use windfalls too early in the season — apple wine should never be made before September — as they tend to be far too high in malic acid and the resultant wine will have a cider taste.

5 lb (2.25 kg) windfall apples
2¼ lb (1.1 kg) sugar
yeast

Wash the apples and remove any decayed parts of the fruit. Chop up, without peeling and immediately add four pints (2 litres) of cold water and a crushed Campden tablet. Cover and allow to stand for twenty four hours, then add the sugar and a vigorous working starter. Note it is essential to use a starter to overcome the residual sterilising effects of the Campden tablet.

After seven days, strain, squeeze and transfer the liquid into a demijohn. Ferment to dryness. Apple wines oxidise far more readily than most and it is essential that all bottles are kept filled and each gallon (4.5 litres) treated with a Campden tablet after each racking.

Variation
Although apple wine has a well developed vinosity all of its own, for those people who enjoy a flowery wine it is possible to develop this characteristic by the addition of half an ounce (15 gm) of either dried elderflower or orange blossom petals. These should be added at the same stage as the sugar.

PLUM WINE

Plums alone produce a wine that is thin. The best way to overcome the problem is to incorporate a pound (0.5 kg) of crushed wheat in every gallon (4.5 litres). Ensure that you buy wheat fit for human consumption. If you can only acquire whole grains, lightly crush with a rolling pin between two layers of cloth. To avoid the dangers of a starch haze forming, amylase — starch enzyme — should be added at the same stage as the pectic enzyme.

4 lb (2 kg) plums
3 lb (1.5 kg) sugar
1 lb (0.5 kg) crushed wheat
1 tsp citric acid
pectic enzyme/starch enzyme
yeast

Remove the stones, which would give the finished wine a woody taste, from the fruit and place together with the sugar and crushed wheat in a bucket. Add five pints (3 litres) of boiling water stirring thoroughly to dissolve the sugar. When cool, add the yeast and enzymes. Allow to stand for ten days, strain and transfer to the demijohn. Keep in a warm place until fermentation ceases. This will give a full bodied medium sweet wine, the colour of which will depend upon the variety of plums chosen.

Plum wine can also be made by the method given for greengages (August).

Variations
Either a pound (0.5 kg) of raisins or sultanas may be used instead of the wheat. Add the dried fruit to the plums.

Small quantities of pure grape juice tend to be lost against the background of the plums. However the liquid obtained by boiling a pound (0.5 kg) of skinned bananas does provide a subtly different wine which is worth making.

PEAR WINE

Pears are not a particularly good fruit for winemaking, but if you have an excess of the fruit use the following ingredients.

5 lb (2.25 kg) pears
2¾ lb (1.25 kgs) sugar
yeast

Make the wine by the same method as given for apple wine.

PERRY

To make a successful perry it is necessary to use perry pears. Today these are only found in a few old orchards. Such fruits are very hard and it is essential that they are pressed. When the pressed juice is obtained, proceed as described under cider.

HEDGEROW WINE

For years a traditional wine was made in the country from the wild fruits that were available. The quality of this wine varied as much as the ingredients used, often it had too much or too little acid and the flavour could be overpowering. However the following combination of fruits yields one of the best country wines.

It is too early to use rosehips as a main ingredient, but here only a small quantity is used for body and the lack of flavour is unnoticeable.

2 lb (1 kg) blackberries
1 lb (0.5 kg) elderberries
2 lb (1 kg) bullace (or plums)
1 lb (0.5 kg) rosehips
2½ lb (1.25 kg) white sugar
4 oz (110 gm) demerara sugar
pectic enzyme
wine yeast

Remove the stalks from the elderberries and rosehips. Crush the blackberries and elderberries in the bucket; pound the rosehips on a breadboard and cut the bullaces in half, before adding to the bucket. Pour the white sugar into the bucket, cover and leave overnight (this will help to draw the juices out of the fruit). Add two pints (1 litre) of boiling water. Stir until the sugar has dissolved then provide a further three pints (1.5 litres) of cold water. At 70°F (21°C) provide the pectic enzyme and yeast. Stir daily. When the initial head has subsided (usually after five to ten days) strain, transfer to a demijohn and top up if necessary. Ferment to dryness, rack and top up with the demerara sugar dissolved in the minimum quantity of water. This wine should be high in alcohol, feed if necessary with 2 ounce (50 gm) portions of white sugar, do not increase the demerara sugar as the maderisation should not be too pronounced. Keep at least a year.

ELDERBERRY AND BLACKBERRY WINES

The amount of elderberries that can be employed to make a gallon (4.5 litres) of wine is restricted to two and at the most three pounds (1 to 1.5 kg) per gallon (4.5 litres) due to the excessive flavour and tannin. Acid similarly sets the limit to the amount of blackberries that may be used. By combining blackberries and elderberries it is possible to raise the total fruit to five pounds (2.5 kg). Raising the concentration in this way results in a wine superior in flavour, body, fruitiness and vinosity to that made from either fruit singularly.

In all recipes requiring the use of both elderberries and blackberries it is essential to extract the juices, if the skins and pips enter the must you will have the worst of both worlds.

Extract the juice by first mashing in a bucket then covering with boiling water. Allow to cool, before straining through muslin into the fermenting bucket. Very gently squeeze the muslin.

DRY ELDERBERRY AND BLACKBERRY WINE

2 lb (1 kg) elderberries
2 lb (1 kg) blackberries
2¾ lb (1.4 kg) sugar
pectic enzyme
yeast

Prepare the fruit as described above, then add the sugar to the warm liquid. Stir until dissolved, providing extra warm water if necessary. Adjust the volume with tap water to one gallon (4.5 litres). At 70°F (21°C) add both the pectic enzyme and yeast. As soon as the initial fermentation subsides transfer to a demijohn. Ferment to dry or medium dry. This wine is ready for drinking in three months.

SWEET ELDERBERRY AND BLACKBERRY WINE

2 lb (1 kg) elderberries
3 lb (1.5 kg) blackberries
1 lb (0.5 kg) sultanas
3¼ lb (1.6 kg) sugar
pectic enzyme
yeast

Prepare the fruit as described above. Scald the sultanas. Add the sultanas and water to the elderberry and blackberry juice. Dissolve two and three quarter pounds (1.4 kg) of sugar in the liquid and make the volume up to one gallon (4.5 litres). At the fermentation temperature provide the pectic enzyme and yeast. After seven to ten days strain the mixture, transfer to a demijohn and fit an air lock. After the first racking feed with four ounces (110 gm) of sugar and sufficient water to return the volume to one gallon (4.5 litres). If when fermentation ceases the wine is not sweet, repeat the feeding procedure until such time as it is. Store the wine for at least nine months before drinking.

Variation
Replace the sultanas with a pound (0.5 kg) of bananas, extract by boiling the peeled fruit from which all signs of decay has been removed with a pint (0.5 litre) of water for twenty minutes. Strain and add the liquor to the fermenting bucket, at the same stage as the sultanas and liquor are added in the above recipe.

BULLACE WINE

4 lb (2 kg) bullaces
3 lb (1.5 kg) sugar
pectic enzyme
yeast

Cut the fruit before placing in the bucket. You will probably find it difficult to remove the stones at this stage. Pour four pints (2 litres) of boiling water on to the fruit then stir in the sugar. Add a further one and a half pints of tap water. At 70°F (21°C) add the pectic enzyme and yeast. After three to four days the stones will have separated from the fruit and sunk to the bottom of the container. Either strain through muslin into a second bucket or carefully remove the stones with the aid of a large spoon. Allow the wine to remain in the bucket for a total of seven to ten days, before transferring to a demijohn and finishing in the usual manner.

OTHER WINES TO MAKE DURING SEPTEMBER

Dried sloe and banana (see January)
Grapefruit, prune, gooseberry, bilberry, pineapple and lychees, raisin and banana, mixed fruit (see February)
Tea, cranberry, dried elderflower, dried orange blossom, dried peach, fig and banana, dried sloe (see March)

Grapefruit, orange, dried rosehip and banana (see April)
Ginger, banana, rhubarb (see May)
Mead (see July)
Grape and raisin, greengage, apple and damson (see August)
Pumpkin, apple and prune (see October)
Rice, raisin, dried prune, dried apricot, dried apricot and banana, date and banana (see November)
Turnip, barley and potato, sultana, banana and elderflower (see December)

W·I·N·E·M·A·K·I·N·G M·O·N·T·H B·Y M·O·N·T·H
OCTOBER

October is the last month when cheap wines can still be made from the fruits of the hedgerows. It is also the time to make cider and wines from grapes.

CRAB APPLE WINE

Crab apples makes a very fine white wine.

4 lb (2 kg) crab apples
1 lb (0.5 kg) sultanas
3 lb (1.5 kg) sugar
½ tsp citric acid
pectic enzyme
yeast

Chop the crab apples and place with the minced sultanas and sugar in a bucket. Cover with five pints (2.5 litres) of boiling water and allow to cool. Add the pectic enzyme, acid and yeast when the temperature has dropped to 70°F (21°C). After three days strain the liquid, squeezing gently. Stir the liquid daily and immediately the initial fermentation has died down transfer to a demijohn, top up with tap water and fit an air lock. Ferment to dryness.

For a sweeter wine, feed with up to eight ounces (250 gm) of sugar, in two ounce (60 gm) portions. As with apple wine a flowery bouquet may be produced by the addition of half an ounce (15 gm) of either dried elderflower or orange blossom. Either should be added at the same stage as the sugar.

As with all types of apple wine, crab apple is prone to oxidation and will develop a light brown colour; to overcome this problem use the method (but not the quantities) described under apple wine page 112.

SLOE WINE

Sloes should be allowed to remain on the bushes as long as is practical in order that the quantities of natural sugars may increase and the harsh acids and tannin, which predominate in the young fruit, may mellow.

2½ lb (1.25 kg) sloes
1 lb (0.5 kg) raisins
2½ lb (1.25 kg) sugar
pectic enzyme
yeast

Put the sloes in a saucepan with two pints (1 litre) of water and bring to the boil. Pour the fruit and the liquid on to the sugar and minced raisins contained in a bucket. Stir thoroughly to dissolve the sugar, mashing the fruit as far as practical during the process. Add a further three pints (1.5 litres) of water and when the temperature has reached 70°F (21°C) add the yeast and pectic enzyme. After two days if using a yeast starter or three days if using dried yeast, but no longer, strain the liquid through muslin, squeezing only very lightly. Transfer to a demijohn. Fit an air lock, but do not top up at this stage, this should not be done until the vigorous initial fermentation has subsided otherwise the liquid will overflow. Keep in the fermentation cabinet until the wine ceases to work.

Variations
The pound (0.5 kg) of raisins may be replaced with an identical amount of wheat.

The addition of the liquid obtained by boiling a pound (0.5 kg) of bananas for twenty minutes to either recipe, greatly increases the body.

For a sweeter wine, feed with up to an extra eight ounces (250 gm) of sugar. If the wine still seems to be harsh to the taste after twelve months, you may add a tablespoonful of glycerine per bottle. Shake to dissolve and leave for one month.

SLOE GIN

Sufficient to make one 26fl oz (70 cl) bottle of one of the finest of our liqueurs which will be ready for drinking this Christmas.

4 oz (110 gm) sloes
4 oz (110 gm) sugar
¼ bottle of gin
red wine to 26 oz (70 cl)

Pick the sloes as late in the season as is practical. If you are forced to gather the fruit early then keep them until they begin to shrivel, but do not allow them to decay. Prick the sloes and place them in the bottom of a wine bottle, together with the sugar and gin. Add the red wine (preferably sloe, but any wine will suffice) to within an inch (2.5 cm) of the shoulder. Do not add more wine as it will make shaking difficult. Keep until Christmas, shaking frequently, and before serving decant into another bottle.

QUINCE OR JAPONICA WINE

Quinces are not very plentiful in this country but the fruit of the chaenomeles japonica (Maule's Quince) which although slightly smaller, is both similar in taste and appearance, may be used. These fruits are ready for winemaking from October to December. Wait until the fruits are yellow before using them.

4 lb (2 kg) quinces or japonica quinces
1 lb (0.5 kg) sultanas
2½ lb (1.25 kg) sugar
1 tsp citric acid
pectic enzyme
yeast

Wash the fruit and remove any decayed pieces, dice but do not peel and bring just to the boil with five pints (2.5 litres) of water. When cool enough to handle safely, pour on to the minced sultanas and sugar. Stir until the sugar has dissolved and make the total volume up to one gallon (4.5 litres). Allow the temperature to reach 70°F (21°C), then add the acid, pectic enzyme and yeast. Allow the fermentation to proceed on the must for ten days, to extract the maximum amount of juice and flavouring from the hard fruit. Strain, transfer to a demijohn, top up, fit an air lock and ferment to dryness.

HAWTHORN WINE

The fruit of the hawthorn may be used to produce a cheap wine, which has a very light flavour. Not one of the best country wines.

4 lb (2 kg) hawthorn
3 lb (1.5 kg) sugar
2 tsp citric acid
yeast

Strip the berries from the stalks and place all the ingredients, with the exception of the yeast, in a fermenting bucket and add six pints (3.5 litres) of water (sufficient boiling water to cover the fruit and the rest as cold water fifteen minutes later). Add the yeast at a temperature of 70°F (21°C). Strain after a fortnight, transfer to a demijohn, top up with tap water and ferment to dryness.

MARROW WINE

This wine is far better than the more traditional marrow rum recipe.

6 lb (3 kg) marrow
1 lb (0.5 kg) sultanas
2¾ lb (1.4 kg) sugar
2 medium sized oranges
1 tsp citric acid
yeast

Take six pounds (3 kg) of peeled and diced marrow (if you do not possess the quantity then a very acceptable wine can be made from four pounds (2 kg) of the fruit, but do not be tempted to use less), and place in the fermenting bucket. Add the minced sultanas, the juice from the oranges — making sure that none of the pith enters the must — and the citric acid. Add the sugar as a syrup dissolved in two pints (1 litre) of water, a further four pints (2 litres) of cold water and the yeast. Leave covered at 70°F (21°C) for ten days. Strain, squeeze the cloth thoroughly and transfer to a demijohn. Rack the wine, which should be sweet, after fermentation is complete.

Variation
Pumpkin may be used instead of marrow.

MEDLAR WINE

4 lb (2 kg) medlar
3 lb (1.5 kg) sugar
1 tsp citric acid
yeast

The fruit should be ripe, but not rotten. Wash, but do not peel, chop the fruit up and place together with all the ingredients, except the yeast, in the fermentation bucket. Add six pints (3 litres) of boiling water, stir thoroughly. Allow the temperature to drop and add the yeast. After a fortnight, strain with gentle squeezing of the cloth and transfer to a demijohn. Ferment to dryness.

ROWANBERRY WINE

Although the fruit of the mountain ash is very plentiful and easy to gather the resultant wine invariably has a bitter taste. But if you still wish to make the wine use the following recipe.

3 lb (1.5 kg) rowanberries
3 lb (1.5 kg) sugar
1 tsp citric acid
yeast

Make the wine by the method given for hawthorn berry wine.

WINES FROM HOME GROWN GRAPES

The best wines come from grapes, indeed strictly speaking the term wine should only be applied to the fermented juice of the grape. What type of wine you produce from your grapes will depend upon many different factors, including the variety of the vine, the type of soil and whether the summer was wet or dry. Nevertheless provided that a little care was taken in its preparation the amateur will be delighted with his wine.

To make one gallon (4.5 litres) of wine requires from ten to fifteen pounds (4.5–7 kg) of grapes. Since few people will possess enough grapes to make a wine containing more than ten pounds (4.5 kg) of grapes, and because it is impractical to make less than a gallon of wine it is best to extract as much juice as possible and to add a small quantity of water and make up to one gallon (4.5 litres). Diluting in this way it is necessary to add some extra sugar, termed chaptalisation, to restore the balance. Due to the vagaries of the climate, it is not possible to know the exact composition of the juice, but most years there will be sufficient acid present, even after the juice has been diluted. If you find when you come to drink the wine that it is slightly bland, then add tartaric acid to taste.

If you intend making more than the occasional gallon (4.5 litres), then a very simple press can be made from a piece of flat wood, of only slightly smaller dimensions than the bucket and fitted with a pole that can be used for moving it up and down. Place the grapes in the bucket and pound with the device. If you wish to make just an experimental gallon (4.5 litres), then the fruit can be mashed with a fork. But to do this so that all the fruit is broken is a very laborious task.

To the crushed grapes and juice in the bucket add one crushed Campden tablet. Cover the bucket with an air-tight lid or plastic film and after twenty-four hours add a vigorously fermenting yeast starter. If you are making a white wine allow to ferment for two days, strain through a strong cloth and squeeze. Make the total up to seven pints (4 litres) with tap water. Remove a small quantity of the liquid and determine the gravity. It is most probable that the gravity will be between 1.040 and 1.050 (you may ignore the small loss of sugar due to the early fermentation). Using this quantity of grapes the optimum starting gravity is 1.080 which will give a finished wine containing about 10% alcohol. Addition of sugar to the must at the rate of five ounces (125 gm) per gallon (4.5 litres) raises the gravity by 0.010, so if your original juice had a gravity of 1.040 then you will require 4×5, i.e. 20 oz (530 gm) of sugar. Dissolve the sugar in the minimum amount of water, transfer with the strained juice to a demijohn, fit an air lock and ferment to dryness. If any air space remains fill with tap water. There are simplifications involved in the calculation of the amount of sugar required, but any error involved does not affect the finished wine. You do not need a degree in mathematics or for that matter science to make good wines.

White wines can also be made from red grapes, if the juice is pressed out and separated from the skins, which alone give colour to the wine. But the best plan with red grapes is to make red wine. Proceed as directed for making white wine, taking the gravity after the second day and adding extra sugar and water. Do not strain nor transfer to a demijohn at this stage. Leave in the bucket for a further seven days, during which time much of the colour and tannin will have been extracted from the skins. Then strain, transfer to the demijohn and ferment to dryness.

If you prefer a rosé wine, then using red grapes make the wine exactly as directed under white wine, separating the juice from the skins after the second day, by which time only a slight amount of colouring will have been extracted.

All the wines described will be dry. The British climate does not lend itself to growing grapes suitable for making sweet wines and if you add extra sugar prior to fermentation the resulting wine will be unbalanced, being far too high in alcohol. Consequently it will have a harsh taste. If you prefer a sweet wine, sweeten by the addition of a sugar syrup solution, adding according to taste, just prior to drinking the wine. Before sweetening the wine add a tablespoonful of glycerine, this will mellow the wine, give it extra body and provide some degree of sweetness.

CIDER

Cider is made entirely from the juice of apples, without the addition of either sugar or water. Commercial producers grow special varieties of apples, but it is possible to make good cider from any apples, providing you possess a press or a liquidiser capable of handling a large quantity of fruit.

Allow the fruit to ripen fully, some people prefer to let the apples fall to the ground, collect, remove any decayed parts and extract the juice.

Four-fifths fill a previously sterilised plastic container with apple juice, a sherry-five is ideal, fitted with an air lock and add a vigorously fermenting bakers yeast starter. This method involves no sterilisation of the must. Infection, although it does occasionally occur, is far less of a problem with cider — provided that you add the yeast starter immediately you have obtained the juice — than any other drink. Perhaps even germs cannot live in a good scrumpy.

APPLE AND PRUNE WINE

The tendency of apples to oxidise when combined with prunes improves rather than detracts from this sherry style wine.

3 lb (1.5 kg) apples
½ lb (250 gm) prunes
2½ lb (1.25 kg) white sugar
6 oz (175 gm) demerara sugar
2 tsp citric acid
pectic enzyme
wine yeast

Soak the prunes in a pint (0.5 litre) of cold water overnight. Remove the stalks and any signs of decay from the apples; cut into thin slices. Cover with boiling water before adding the prunes and the water in which they were soaked. Add the white sugar and a further three pints (1.5 litres) of hot water. Stir until the sugar has dissolved. Add sufficient cold water to make the total up to one gallon (4.5 litres). At 70°F (21°C) add acid, yeast and pectic enzyme. Stir daily. As soon as the stones separate from the fruit, strain into a second bucket or remove the stones with a spoon or other suitable implement. When the initial fermentation has subsided, strain, gently squeeze and transfer to a demijohn. Top up if necessary and ferment to dryness. Rack and feed with 3 ounces (80 gm) of demerara sugar dissolved in sufficient water to return to the original volume. Ferment to dryness and repeat the process. Allow the wine which will be a rich cream sherry style to mature for at least a year.

PUMPKIN WINE

5 lb (2.5 kg) pumpkin pieces
1 lb (0.5 kg) sultanas
2¾ lb (1.4 kg) white sugar
6 oz (175 gm) demerara sugar
2 lemons or
2 tsp citric acid
yeast

Dice the pumpkin and place in a bucket with the white sugar, cover the bucket and leave for one week. Cover a pound (0.5 kg) of sultanas with a pint (0.5 litre) of boiling water. Strain the liquid from the pumpkin and sugar on to the sultanas. Make up to one gallon (4.5 litre) with tap water before adding the acid and the yeast. Place in a warm area and ferment for ten days, before transferring to a demijohn and fitting an airlock. Ferment to dryness and feed with three ounces (80 gm) of demerara sugar. Repeat the process with white sugar if the wine is still not sweet. This slightly maderised wine is ready for drinking after a year and will improve for a further two years.

OTHER WINES TO MAKE DURING OCTOBER

Dried sloe and banana (see January)
Grapefruit, prune, gooseberry, bilberry, pineapple, lychees, mixed fruit, raisin and banana (see February)
Tea, cranberry, dried elderberry, dried elderflower, dried orange blossom, dried peach, fig and banana, dried sloe (see March)
Grapefruit, orange, dried rosehip and banana (see April)
Ginger, banana (see May)
Apple and damson (see August)
Bullace (see September)
Rice, dried prune, dried date, dried apricot, dried apricot and banana, date and banana, rosehip and apple, rosehip and parsnip (see November)
Sultana, banana and elderflower (see December)

W·I·N·E·M·A·K·I·N·G M·O·N·T·H B·Y M·O·N·T·H
NOVEMBER

There is very little fresh material for winemaking during November. In some years sloes will remain on the bushes and if you are lucky enough to find them they are at their best for our purpose.

Rosehips and roots are available at this time of the year but neither as yet are really ready.

However, some excellent wines can be made from dried fruit at this time, or indeed any time of the year.

DATE AND BANANA WINE

½ lb (250 gm) slab of dates
2 lb (1 kg) ripe bananas
2¾ lb (1.4 kg) sugar
2 tsp citric acid
starch enzyme (amylase)
yeast

Break the dates up into small pieces and place in the fermentation bucket. Boil the bananas for 20 minutes and pour the liquid and solid on to the dates. Add the acid and make up to one gallon (4.5 litres) with tap water. At fermentation temperature add the yeast and amylase.

Ferment in the usual manner to make a medium sweet tawny wine which needs keeping for a further month and which will benefit from twice this storage period.

NOTE: Due to the strong flavour of the dates, fermentation may be conducted in the presence of bananas. This brings about a complete extraction of the fruit.

DATE WINE

1 lb (0.5 kg) stoneless dates
1 lb (0.5 kg) sultanas or raisins
2 lb (1 kg) sugar
1½ tsp citric acid
pectic enzyme
yeast

Mince the sultanas and break up the dates (do not try to put them through the mincer). Cover with two pints (1 litre) of boiling water and add the sugar dissolved in another two pints (1 litre) of hot water. Add the citric acid and lower the temperature by the addition of a further three pints (1.5 litres) of cold water. When the temperature has dropped to 70°F (21°C) add the yeast and pectic enzyme. Stir daily, after a fortnight transfer to a demijohn, top up with water, fit an air lock and keep in the fermentation cupboard until no further bubbles are seen to escape from the air lock.

Variation
Replace the sultanas with a pound (0.5 kg) of crushed wheat. Using this ingredient it is necessary to increase the acid to 2 tsp and to add starch enzyme (amylase) at the same stage as the pectic enzyme. The dominant flavour comes from the dates and there is very little difference in the finished wine whether sultanas or raisins are used.

DRIED APRICOT WINE

This is one of the most economical of all wines, because after some of the flavour has been extracted, the apricots may be used for normal culinary purposes.

2 lb (1 kg) dried apricots
1 lb (0.5 kg) sultanas
3 lb (1.5 kg) sugar
2 tsp citric acid
pectic enzyme
yeast

Soak the dried fruit overnight in two–three pints (1–1.5 litres) of water in a saucepan. Next day bring the apricots and water to the boil and simmer until the fruit is soft. Cool. Decant off the liquid, this will be used for making the wine and the now soft fruit may be used to make a pie.

Mince the sultanas and place in a bucket with the sugar and four pints (2 litres) of boiling water. To this mixture add the liquid from the apricots, make up to one gallon (4.5 litres) and when the temperature is at 70°F (21°C) add the yeast and pectic enzyme. After seven days, strain, transfer to a demijohn, top up with water and ferment to dryness.

DRIED APRICOT AND BANANA WINE

Replace the sultanas in the above recipe with a pound and a half (0.75 kg) of very ripe bananas. Skin and remove any signs of decay. Leave standing in the refrigerator for four days before use. Add the bananas to the dried apricots.

Alternatively you may extract the juice from the bananas by simmering for twenty minutes with a pint (0.5 litres) of water.

ROSEHIP AND APPLE WINE

Whilst it is still too early to use rosehips as the sole ingredient, they may be profitably employed in a blended must.

1 lb (0.5 kg) rosehips
1lb (0.5 kg) apples
1 lb (0.5 kg) bananas
2¾ lb (1.4 kg) white sugar
4 oz (110 gm) demerara sugar
1½ tsp citric acid
pectic enzyme
yeast

Crush the rosehips, chop up the apples and peel the bananas then place the three main ingredients in the bucket. Add the three pounds of white sugar and four pints of boiling water. Stir until the sugar dissolves. Add sufficient water (about 2½ pints) to make up to one gallon (4.5 litres). Provide acid, yeast and pectic enzyme.

After seven days transfer to a demijohn. Fit an airlock. Ferment to dryness. Rack.

Feed with four ounces (110 gm) of demerara sugar dissolved in sufficient water to return the total volume to one gallon (4.5 litres). If further feeding is necessary to produce a sweet wine use white sugar. This maderised dessert needs a year to mature.

DRIED PRUNE WINE

2 lb (1 kg) dried prunes
1 lb (0.5 kg) sultanas
3 lb (1.5 kg) sugar
2 tsp citric acid
pectic enzyme
yeast

Prepare the wine by the same method as that described for dried apricot wine, again using prunes for culinary uses after the flavouring has been extracted. The resultant wine, which will have a sherry flavour, should be of medium sweetness. This can be increased by feeding with 2 ounce (50 gm) portions of white sugar. Addition of one teaspoonful of glycerine per bottle will increase the body of the wine.

SWEET RAISIN WINE

All raisin wines are very good, but the flavour will depend upon the type of raisins used. It is a good idea to taste the fruit first and only use the muscatel raisins, which give a finished wine similar to a madeira.

2 lb (1 kg) raisins
2 lb (1 kg) sugar
1 tsp citric acid
pectic enzyme
yeast

Liquidise or mince the raisins, taking care not to crush the seeds. Place in a bucket with the sugar and citric acid. Add six pints (3 litres) of boiling water and stir until the sugar has dissolved. When the temperature has dropped to 70°F (21°C) add both the yeast and pectic enzyme. After the initial head has subsided, strain the liquid through muslin, make up to a gallon (4.5 litres) and place in a demijohn. Top up with water and fit an air lock. If the wine tastes sweet it may be bottled, but if it is dry (since the amount of sugar varies with the raisin type and it is not possible to give more exact details), then half a pound (250 gm) of sugar dissolved in a quarter pint (150 ml) of water should be added after the final racking and the wine refermented.

Variation
The addition of orange blossom petals at the rate of half an ounce (15 gm) per gallon (4.5 litres) produces a flowery wine which is ideal for drinking at any time, but especially as a sweet aperitif.
The addition of elderflowers to the wine is far less successful.

RICE WINE

2 lb (1 kg) rice
1 lb (0.5 kg) sultanas
3 lb (1.5 kg) sugar
2 tsp citric acid
pectic enzyme/starch enzyme
yeast

Rice is very high in starch, so to ensure that the wine clears it is important to use both starch and pectic enzymes.

Place the minced sultanas and the rice in a bucket, add four pints (2 litres) of boiling water and stir in the sugar which should dissolve readily. Add a further two pints (1 litre) of cold water and allow the temperature to reach 70°F (21°C) then add the yeast and both pectic and starch enzymes together with the acid. After the initial vigorous fermentation has ceased, usually this takes about ten days, strain and transfer to a demijohn. Fit an air lock and ferment to dryness.

WHEAT WINE

1 lb (0.5 kg) wheat
1 lb (0.5 kg) raisins
3 lb (1.5 kg) sugar
2½ tsp citric acid
pectic enzyme/starch enzyme
yeast

It is easier to use crushed wheat, but if you can only obtain whole grains sandwich it between a cloth and crush with a rolling pin. Do not crush to a fine powder as this may cause problems with the clearing of the wine — breaking the grains in half is sufficient. Buy seedless raisins, the fuller flavour is preferable to sultanas (although these may be used) within this particular wine.

Place the crushed wheat, sugar and acid in the fermentation bucket, cover with six pints (3 litres) of boiling water and ensure that the sugar dissolves.

At 70°F (21°C) add the yeast and both pectic and starch enzymes as the main ingredients contain both pectin and starch. After ten days strain and treat in the usual way.

This gives a dessert wine that benefits from keeping for up to two years.

ROSEHIP AND PARSNIP WINE

A nutty sherry style wine can be made from

1 lb (0.5 kg) rosehips
2 lb (1.0 kg) parsnips
½ lb (250 gm) sultanas
3 lb (1.5 kg) sugar
2 tsp citric acid
amylase
yeast

Boil the parsnips with two pints (1.0 litre) of water and simmer for twenty minutes before straining the liquid on to the crushed rosehips and sultanas. Discard the parsnips or use for culinary purposes. Add the sugar and four pints (2.0 litres) of warm water, stir until dissolved before providing a further two pints (1 litre) of cold water. Check that the temperature is in the 65-70°F (18.5-21°C) range before adding the citric acid, amylase and wine yeast. Stir daily when the initial fermentation has subsided, strain and transfer to a demijohn, topping up if necessary. Ferment to dryness.

After racking, divide the liquid in two and place each half in separate demijohns. Fit cotton wool plugs in each container. Store for one month at room temperature and then recombine. This oxidised wine may be drunk immediately and it keeps for about eighteen months.

To increase the body and smoothness of the wine, add a teaspoonful of glycerine to each bottle immediately after the final racking.

OTHER WINES TO MAKE DURING NOVEMBER

Carrot, parsnip, potato, wheat and potato, fig and rosehip, dried sloe and banana, swede (see January)
Grapefruit, prune, gooseberry, bilberry, pineapple, lychees, mixed fruit, raisin and banana, prune and parsnip (see February)
Tea, cranberry, dried elderberry, dried elderflower, dried orange blossom, dried peach, fig and banana, dried sloe (see March)
Orange, grapefruit, dried rosehip and banana (see April)
Ginger, banana (see May)
Pumpkin, apple and prune (see October)
Turnip, barley and potato, sultana, banana and elderflower (see December)

DECEMBER

December is a month for drinking wine rather than making it, there being very little cheap fruit available, although stocks can be replenished by fermenting roots, tinned and dried fruits. It is the time for parties, when liqueurs and punches are the order of the day.

LIQUEUR MAKING

Liqueur making differs from other types of home drink making in two ways. First, they are ready for drinking immediately they are mixed, there being no fermentation stage, and secondly at least some of the alcohol has to be purchased. Nevertheless they are still considerably cheaper than their commercial counterparts, but at only 18-22 per cent they are seldom as strong. Apart from the savings there are two other major advantages of making your own liqueurs. It is possible, with just a little experimentation, to design a drink to suit your palate, and having a lower alcohol content more can be drunk.

When making liqueurs you may either rely on the standard recipes, which will give you a smooth full drink, or you can adjust the amounts of the various ingredients to bring out the particular characteristic that you want. If you wish to make the drink sweeter, remembering that liqueurs are usually very sweet anyway as they are designed to suppress the appetite at the end of a meal, increase the amount of sugar syrup by a further two fluid ounces (50 ml), per bottle. For higher alcohol strengths the vodka or brandy may be increased by up to twelve fluid ounces (300 ml), but the large increase in cost for only slight improvement in quality cannot really be justified. Where extra alcohol or sugar syrup is used the quantity of wine used in making the liqueur should be decreased by the corresponding amount.

The sugar syrup solution used in all the recipes is made by dissolving two pounds (1 kg) of sugar in a pint (0.5 litre) of water. Smaller quantities can be made pro rata.

The quantities of ingredients given will not completely fill the bottle, but will leave sufficient room to shake easily.

Unlike wines, liqueurs are fairly stable in air and due to their high sugar and alcohol content they may be kept for a reasonable period of time in a partly filled bottle.

DORSET MINT CHOCOLATE LIQUEUR

4 fl oz (100 ml) vodka
6 fl oz (150 ml) sugar syrup
1–2 tbs glycerine
14 fl oz (350 ml) white homemade wine
chocolate essence
peppermint essence
green edible colouring

Use the essence sold in supermarkets for flavouring. With this recipe there is no need to buy special liqueur flavourings.

Place all the ingredients, except the essences but including one tablespoonful of glycerine in a standard twenty-six ounce (70 cl) wine bottle and shake. Then add six drops of the peppermint flavouring and taste, (the best part of the whole procedure). If the liqueur is too thin for your palate, add the second tablespoonful of glycerine, extra peppermint flavouring may also be added if necessary. Now add the chocolate essence to taste. The liqueur may be drunk immediately, but it does improve if left a day for the ingredients to marry together. Some people prefer the liqueur without the addition of the chocolate flavouring. It is up to you to decide — you pay your money and you take your choice.

CHERRY BRANDY TYPE LIQUEUR

4 fl oz (100 ml) brandy
4 fl oz (100 ml) sugar syrup
2 tbs glycerine
14 fl oz (350 ml) red homemade wine
1 bottle cherry brandy flavouring

Place all the ingredients in a twenty-six ounce (70 cl) bottle; shake thoroughly. Sample a liqueur glass of the mixture. If you feel that it requires more alcohol add a further two fluid ounces (50 ml) of brandy. The sweetness may be increased by adding the same quantity of sugar syrup. Make small additions, tasting at all stages. Remember you can always add extra amounts, but you cannot take them away.

OTHER LIQUEURS

There is a whole range of liqueur flavourings on the market and these produce very good drinks if added to either of the basic recipes, minus the flavourings, given under Dorset Mint Chocolate Liqueur or Cherry Brandy Type Liqueur. Decide whether vodka or brandy is the more appropriate additive and select the appropriate recipe.

BLACKBERRY OR PEACH LIQUEUR

14 fl oz (350 ml) sweet blackberry or sweet peach wine
4 fl oz (100 ml) sugar syrup
4 fl oz (100 ml) brandy

Shake and mix the ingredients thoroughly, then serve.

Theoretically it should be possible to make a cheap liqueur using any wine in this way, but the only wines that are really suitable are blackberry and peach.

ROSEHIP WINE

By December the frost will have broken down the rosehips, and the birds will not have started eating them yet.

It is the only ingredient that is really at its best for winemaking during this month.

4 lb (2 kg) rosehips
3 lb (1.5 kg) sugar
2 tsp citric acid
yeast

Clean the rosehips thoroughly by leaving them to soak in a bucket of water overnight, pour off the water, add the sugar and six pints (3 litres) of boiling water and allow to cool. When the temperature has dropped to 70°F (21°C) add the yeast and citric acid.

Ferment on the must for five days. Strain the liquid through muslin, transfer to a demijohn, top up with water and ferment to dryness. Should you wish, the wine may be sweetened to taste.

PUNCH

A warming glass of punch, when your guests arrive, is essential to any party. There can be few punches better, or cheaper, than those made from country wines. The quantities given below are sufficient for forty servings.

3 bottles of red wine
1 cup of orange squash (undiluted)
3 tots cheap brandy, whisky or vodka (optional)
3 tbs of glycerine
1 tsp mixed spices
½ tsp cinnamon
12 cloves
sugar to taste (made by dissolving 2 lb (1 kg) of sugar in 1 pint (0.75 litre) of water)

The quality of the punch is greatly improved by the addition of the three tots of spirits, but should you wish to omit these you will still have a very enjoyable warming drink to start the evening off with a swing.

Place the wine, orange squash, glycerine and the spirits in a saucepan. Heat to 160°F (71°C) but no higher as most of the alcohol will evaporate.

Remove from the heat and add the spices and sugar syrup. Depending upon the nature of the wine used you may not need all of the spices. Make frequent testings until you are satisfied with the punch. It is important that you adjust the flavour at the temperature you intend serving the drink. You may reheat if necessary, but do not exceed the maximum recommended temperature.

If you do not possess a punch bowl a little ingenuity can overcome the problem. Fruit bowls or earthenware dishes, which can if necessary be covered in crepe paper, can be used as punch bowls. Floating a sliced orange on the drink improves the presentation of your bowl and adds a little flavour to the drink.

If you have insufficient homemade wine, replace with an equal quantity of cider and add pieces of chopped apple to the punch bowl.

Serve the punch either in pyrex cups or wine glasses, and allow approximately two fluid ounces (50 ml) per guest for the first serving — but be warned, they will come back for more.

SULTANA, BANANA AND ELDERFLOWER WINE

This is not a flower wine, but rather a fruit wine with just the subtlest trace of flowery bouquet. Correctly made no one should realise that it does contain any elderflowers. Made at this time of the year it should serve as a reminder of what should be the new year's resolution of all home brewers, "To be a little more adventurous with my winemaking."

1½ lb (0.75 kg) sultanas
2 lb (1 kg) bananas
2¼ lb (1.1 kg) sugar
¼ oz (7 gm) dried elderflowers
2 tsp citric acid
yeast

Place the peeled bananas in a container in the freezer, or freezing compartment of the refrigerator 48 hours before they are required. Add the bananas together with any liquid which may have come out of them to the sultanas and elderflowers in a fermentation bucket. Cover with 4 pints (2 litres) of boiling water. Pour in the sugar, stir until it has dissolved. Add a further 2¾ pints (1.5 litres) of cold water. At 70°F (21°C) provide the yeast and citric acid. Stir daily. Strain after seven days, pour into a demijohn and fit an air lock. The wine which should be medium sweet may be drunk in nine months to one year's time.

Variation
During June or July you may use the petals from one medium sized elderflower head.

ORANGE GIN

To make approximately four bottles of this imitation orange gin you will require

1¾ pints (1 litre) pure orange juice
2½ lb (1.25 kg) sugar
4 tbs glycerine
½–1 bottle of gin (see below)
1 medium sized orange
pectic enzyme
yeast

The principle employed in making this mock liqueur is to prepare the strongest orange wine possible and to add sugar syrup, glycerine and gin to produce a drink in the 20 per cent plus alcohol range.

Place the one and three quarter pints (1 litre) of orange juice and one and a half pounds (1.25 kg) sugar in a demijohn. Add one pint (0.5 litre) of water, the pectic enzyme and the wine yeast. Do not top up to one gallon (4.5 litres). When the initial fermentation has subsided transfer to a half gallon (2–3 litre) demijohn (or whisky jar). Ferment to dryness and feed with additional sugar syrup until the maximum alcohol level is reached. Taste the wine to ensure that it is sound. Never attempt to add spirit to an unsound wine.

Pour the wine on to the zest of one medium sized orange. Store for one month. Taste. The wine should be sweet with a pronounced orange flavour. Pour into a gallon (4.5 litres) demijohn. Add one pound (0.5 kg) of sugar dissolved in half a pint (250 ml) of water. Add half to a full bottle of gin, making small additions, shaking and tasting after each addition. The more spirit that you provide the better will be the liqueur. Bottle. It is possible to increase the body of the orange gin by the addition of a tablespoon of glycerine per bottle. This is not essential.

If you are prepared to add a full bottle of gin, you may blend to obtain a balance with respect to sweetness. This is achieved by adding the bottle of gin to the wine, and adding the sugar syrup solution (one pound (0.5 kg) of sugar to half a pint (250 ml) of water) until the correct degree of sweetness is achieved. This results in a slightly better liqueur.

BARLEY AND POTATO WINE

2 lb (1 kg) potatoes
1 lb (0.5 kg) crushed barley
2½ lb (1.25 kg) white sugar
½ lb (250 gm) demerara sugar
2 tsp citric acid
starch enzyme (amylase)
yeast

Use only barley that is sold for human consumption. It is essential when making this particular wine to add starch enzyme — amylase. Prepare the potatoes as described under potato wine. Crush the barley by sandwiching between two layers of tea towel and pounding with a rolling pin. Place both in the fermentation bucket, add the white sugar and demerara sugar together with the acid. Cover with four pints (2 litres) of boiling water and make up to a total of one gallon (4.5 litres) with tap water. At 70°F (21°C) provide both the yeast and amylase. After seven to ten days transfer to a demijohn; top up if necessary and fit an air lock. Ferment, with rackings until the evolution of bubbles ceases. If necessary feed to produce a sweeter wine.

TURNIP WINE

Turnip wine is one of the oldest of all country wines. In the original method, turnips were crushed in a cider press. It was the liquid so obtained that the sugar and raisins were added to. This method must have been very costly in terms of roots used, as turnips yield only small quantities of liquid. The modern method is to extract the flavour with water and alcohol by fermenting on the must.

4 lb (2 kg) turnips
1 lb (0.5 kg) sultanas
3 lb (1.5 kg) white sugar
2 oranges
1 tsp citric acid
starch enzyme (amylase)
yeast

Peel and dice the turnips; place in a fermenting bucket with the sultanas and the juice from two medium sized oranges. Add the sugar and two pints (1 litre) of boiling water. Stir until all solid has dissolved, then make up to a gallon (4.5 litres) with cold water. Add the enzyme, acid and yeast. Stir daily, strain and transfer to a demijohn. After the initial fermentation has subsided, rack as necessary. The wine which needs a nine month maturation period should be a medium sweet social grade.

OTHER WINES TO MAKE DURING DECEMBER

Parsnip, carrot, potato, wheat and potato, fig and rosehip, dried sloe and banana, swede (see January)
Grapefruit, prune, gooseberry, bilberry, pineapple, lychees, mixed fruit, raisin and banana, prune and parsnip (see February)
Tea, cranberry, dried elderflower, dried elderberry, dried orange blossom, dried peach, fig and banana, dried sloe (see March)
Grapefruit, orange, dried rosehip and banana (see April)
Ginger, banana (see May)
Pumpkin, apple and prune (see October)
Rice, raisin, dried date, dried prune, dried apricot, dried apricot and banana, date and banana, rosehip and apple, rosehip and parsnip (see November)

Wine		Recipe on Page	Months During Which the Wine May be Made (JAN–DEC)	Shortest	Optimum	Type of Wine	Alcohol %
Apple	****	112		12	18	tab/soc/cul	12–15
Apple and Damson		101		4	9	soc	14
Apple and Prune	***	125		12	24	ap/soc	15
Apricot (fresh)	***	103		9	18	soc	14
Apricot (dried)	***	128		12	18	soc	14
Banana	***	76		9	24	soc/des	13–15
Barley and Potato	***	138		12	18		15
Beetroot	***	99		12	24	des	16
Bilberry	***	110		3	12	tab/soc	14
Bilberry Claret	*****	111		3	12	tab/cul	10–12
Bilberry Port	*****	109		6	24	des	16
Bilberry I (canned)	*****	51		3	24	tab/soc	12
Bilberry II (canned)	***	52		3	24	tab/soc	12
Bilberry and Blackberry (dry)	*****	111		5	9	tab/cul	10–12
Bilberry and Blackberry (sweet)	****	110		12	18	soc	14–16
Birch Sap	***	57		9	18	tab/cul	12–13
Blackberry	****	106		3	6	tab/soc/cul	12
Blackberry Claret	*****	107		3	6	tab/cul	10–12
Blackberry Port	*****	106		12	24	des	16+
Blackberry and Sultana	****	107		9	18	soc	14
Blackcurrant	****	85		12	18	soc	14
Bramble Tip	**	74		12	18	tab	12–14
Bullace	***	116		6	9	soc	14
Burnet		86		6	12	soc/tab	12
Carrot	***	44		12	24	soc	15–16
Cherry	***	84		12	18	tab/soc	14
Coltsfoot	***	66		6	12	tab	12
Crab Apple	***	119		12	24	soc	14–15
Cranberry (frozen)	***	61		9	12	tab/soc	14
Damson	***	99		12	18	des	15–16+
Dandelion	***	65		12	18	tab/soc	13–14
Date	***	128		12	24	soc/des	13–14
Date and Banana	***	127		6	12	soc/des	14
Elderberry	****	108		3	12	tab/cul	13
Elderberry Burgundy	*****	109		3	12	tab/cul	10–12
Elderberry Port	*****	108		3	12	des	16+
Elderberry (dried) I	***	59		12	24	tab	10
Elderberry (dried) II	***	59		12	12	tab	12

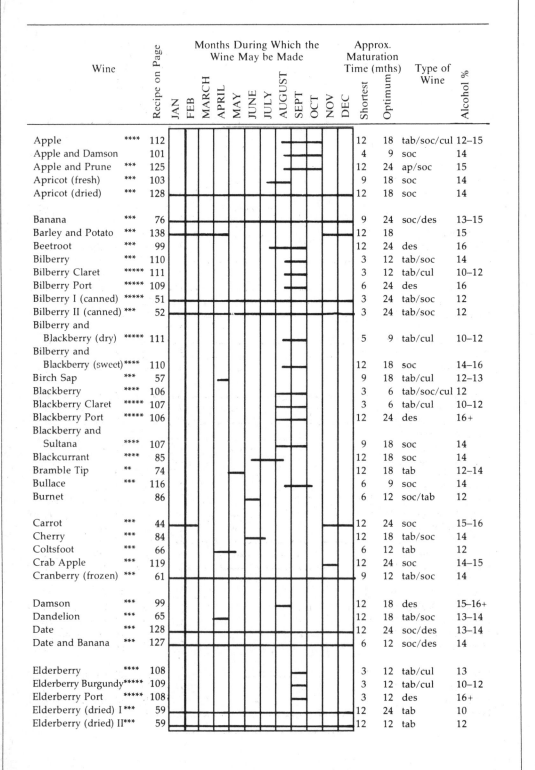

Wine		Recipe on Page	JAN	FEB	MARCH	APRIL	MAY	JUNE	JULY	AUGUST	SEPT	OCT	NOV	DEC	Shortest	Optimum	Type of Wine	Alcohol %
Elderberry and Blackberry (dry)	*****	115									—				3	9	tab/cul	13–14
Elderberry and Blackberry (sweet)	*****	115									—				9	18	des	16
Elderflower – Modern	****	80						—							6 wks	3	tab	8–11
Elderflower – Traditional	*****	79						—							6	12	tab/soc/cul	14
Elderflower (dried)	****	60						—							12	18	tab/cul	13
Exotic Fruit Wines	****	50	—	—	—	—	—	—	—	—	—	—	—	—	6 wks	3	tab/soc	10
Fruit Juice	****	52	—	—	—	—	—	—	—	—	—	—	—	—	6 wks	6	tab/soc	12–13
Fig and Banana	****	62	—	—	—	—	—	—	—	—	—	—	—	—	12	18	des	16
Fig and Rosehip	*****	47	—	—	—	—	—	—	—	—	—	—	—	—	12	24	soc/des	14–15
Guavas (canned)	****	50	—	—	—	—	—	—	—	—	—	—	—	—	6 wks	6	tab/soc	12
Ginger	**	77	—	—	—	—	—	—	—	—	—	—	—	—	12	24	soc	13
Gooseberry	*****	94							—						6	12	des	16+
Gooseberry (canned) I	*****	49	—	—	—	—	—	—	—	—	—	—	—	—	6wks	3	tab	8–10
Gooseberry (canned) II	*****	50	—	—	—	—	—	—	—	—	—	—	—	—	6wks	3	tab	11–12
Gooseberry and Blackcurrant	***	95							—						9	12	soc	14
Gooseberry and Elderflower	*****	94							—						6	9	tab/cul	13
Gorse or Broom	***	67				——	—	—							6	12	tab/soc	12–13
Grape	*****	123										—			12	24	tab/soc/des	8–16
Grape Prunings	****	100							—	—					12	18	soc	13–14
Grape and Raisin	****	101								—					12	24	ap	15
Grapefruit Fresh	****	69	—	—	—	—	—	—	—	—	—	—	—	—	9	12	tab/ap	13
Grapefruit (canned)	*****	51	—	—	—	—	—	—	—	—	—	—	—	—	6wks	6	tab	12
Grapefruit (juice)	*****	52	—	—	—	—	—	—	—	—	—	—	—	—	6wks	6	tab	12–13
Hawthorn	**	121										—			12	24	soc	14
Hawthorn Blossom	**	76				—									12	18	tab/soc	13–14
Hedgerow Wine	****	114									—				12	24	des	16
Herb (general)	**	130				—	—								6	18	tab/soc/ap	11–12
Honeysuckle	***	92						—	—						12	18	soc	14
Lettuce	*	82					—	—							12	18	tab/soc	10–12
Lime Petal	**	93						—							9	12	tab	12
Loganberry	***	83						—	—						6	18	tab/soc	13–14
Lychees (canned)	***	50	—	—	—	—	—	—	—	—	—	—	—	—	6wks	6	tab/soc	12–13

Wine	Recipe on Page	Months During Which the Wine May be Made	Shortest	Optimum	Type of Wine	Alcohol %
Marrow ***	122		9	18	soc	13–14
Mead Dry *****	91		24	up to	ap/soc	14
Mead Sweet *****	89		24	7 yrs	ap/des	15
Mead, Poor Man's I ***	90		24	48	ap/soc	15
Mead, Poor Man's II***	90		18	24	ap/soc	13
Medlar ***	122		12	18	soc	14
Mixed Fruit ***	54		6	9	tab/soc	12–13
Nettle **	74		9	15	soc	13
Oak Leaf ***	82		12	15	soc	13
Orange (fresh) ***	69		9	12	tab/cul	13
Orange (Seville) ***	46		6wks	6	tab/cul	12
Orange (juice) *****	52		6wks	6	tab/cul	12–13
Orange Blossom (dried) ***	60		6wks	6	tab/cul	13
Parsley ***	81		6	12	soc	13–14
Parsnip ****	43		12	24	soc/des	15
Parsnip (Sherry) ****	43		12	24	soc/ap/cul	15–16
Peach ****	100		12	24	soc/des	14–15
Peach (canned) ***	50		6wks	6	soc/des	12
Peach (dried)	61		6	9	soc	13–14
Pear ***	113		18	24	tab/soc//cul	13
Pea Pod ***	91		12	24	tab/soc/cul	13
Pea Pod and Elderflower ***	91		6	18	soc/cul	13
Pineapple (canned) ****	50		6wks	3	tab/soc	12–13
Pineapple (juice) ****	52		6wks	6	tab/soc	12–13
Plum ***	113		24	24+	soc/des	15
Potato ***	45		18	30	soc/des	15
Prune (canned) ****	53		12	24	des	15–16+
Prune (dried) ****	130		3	9	soc/des/cul	14
Prune and Parsnip *****	54		12	18	ap/soc	16+
Pumpkin ***	126		12	18	soc	15
Quince ***	121		12	24	soc	14–15+
Raisin ****	130		12	24	des	14–15
Raisin and Banana ***	55		9	18	des	16+
Raspberry ****	83		12	18	tab/soc	14
Raspberry Dessert ***	86		12	24	des	15+
Red Currant ***	97		4	18	tab	12
Rhubarb ****	73		6	12	tab/soc	14

The "Months During Which the Wine May be Made" column is divided into: JAN, FEB, MARCH, APRIL, MAY, JUNE, JULY, AUGUST, SEPT, OCT, NOV, DEC. The "Approx. Maturation Time (mths)" column is divided into Shortest and Optimum.

Wine		Recipe on Page	Months During Which the Wine May be Made												Approx. Maturation Time (mths) Shortest	Optimum	Type of Wine	Alcohol %
			JAN	FEB	MARCH	APRIL	MAY	JUNE	JULY	AUGUST	SEPT	OCT	NOV	DEC				
Rhubarb and Elderflower	*****	74						———							6	12	tab/cul	14
Rhubarb Champagne	*****	93					———								6	12	soc/ap	14
Rose Hip	****	135										———			9	15	soc/ap	13
Rose Hip (dried) and Banana	*****	70	————————————————————————————												12	24	des	16
Rose Hip and Parsnip	****	132	———															
Rose Petal	*****	80						———							6	18	tab/soc/cul	12–13
Rose Petal Rosé	****	85						———							9	12	tab	12–13
Rowanberry	**	123									———				9	15	soc	13
Sloe	***	120										———			12	24	soc/des	15
Sloe (dried)	**	62	————————————————————————————												12	18	soc	14–15
Sloe (dried) and Banana	**	47	————————————————————————————												12	18	soc	14
Strawberry	***	83							———						6	12	soc	13
Sultana, Banana and Elderflower	***	137	————————————————————————————												9	12	soc/tab	12–13
Swede	**	46	———												12	18	soc/des	14–15
Tea	***	58	————————————————————————————												12	24	soc/ap	14
Tropical Fruit	***	102	————————————————————————————												12	24	soc	13–14
Turnip		139	———									———			9	18	soc/des	14
Wallflower		75					———								16	19	soc/tab	14
Wheat	***	131							———						24	36	des	16+
White Currant	*****	98						———							12	24	des	16+

The percentage alcohol and maturation times are only approximate — absolute values will differ with the year and the individual winemaker — and should only be used as a guide.

*****	the very best country wines	tab	table wines
****	very good	soc	social wines
***	good, well worth making	des	dessert wines
**	not worth making	ap	aperitif
*	poor	cul	wines recommended for culinary purposes

E·X·O·T·I·C, N·O·V·E·L·T·Y AND O·T·H·E·R W·I·N·E·S

The ingredients given in the winemaking calendar are commonly available throughout the world; the months quoted for the fruits being in season refer to the temperate regions of Europe and North America. Seasons will differ in the tropics and in the Southern Hemisphere, but the time that any plant is fruiting, if not known, can be found in any botanical book.

There are certain fruits which can only be obtained at an economic price in their country of origin. Many of these are ideal for our purpose and it is well worth making wines from these fruits if you are lucky enough to have access to a supply. Particularly fortunate are winemakers living in Australia and North America, for in addition to possessing most of the ingredients of the temperate regions, due to the large size of the country and consequent changes in the climate, tropical fruits are also abundant.

CITRUS WINE

Fresh satsumas, tangerines, clementines, mandarins, ugli fruit and grapefruit may all be used to make excellent dry table wine. This wine is strongly recommended.

2 lb (1 kg) citrus fruit,
if using grapefruit 4 large ones
½ can of grape juice concentrate or
1 lb (0.5 kg) sultanas
2¼ lb (1 kg) sugar
pectic enzyme
yeast

Remove and discard the peel from the fruit. Break the fruit into segments and add to the sugar in the fermenting bucket. Cover with six pints (3 litres) of boiling water. When the temperature has dropped to 70°F (21°C) add the grape juice concentrate, yeast and pectic enzyme. If you use minced sultanas, which are not such a good additive to this light wine, they should be placed in the fermenting bucket with the sugar and fruit segments. Stir the wine daily, mashing the fruit against the sides of the bucket. Strain after a week, transfer to a demijohn and top up with water. Fit an air lock.
NOTE: Occasionally citrus fruit are encountered which have a higher than usual acid level. Should a previous wine have been slightly high in acid reduce the weight of fruit by a quarter.

CACTUS WINE

The prickly pear, the purple fruit of certain opuntias found in Australia and the Americas produces a wine with a characteristic taste which makes it well worth drinking apart from any novelty value cactus wine may possess.

When picking prickly pears always wear gloves as the minute hairlike spines are extremely painful if they enter the bare skin.

4 lb (2 kg) prickly pears
3 lb (1.5 kg) sugar
2 tsp citric acid
1 cup of cold tea
pectic enzyme
yeast

Rub the spines off the fruit with the gloved hand, then peel and dice the fruit. Place in the fermenting bucket with the sugar and cover with six pints (3 litres) of boiling water. When the temperature has dropped to 70°F (21°C) add the citric acid, cold tea, yeast and pectic enzyme. After a week strain, transfer to a demijohn, top up with water and add an air lock.

If you wish to make a fuller bodied wine include half a pound (250 gm) of minced sultanas. These should be placed in the bucket together with the fruit and sugar. If you include sultanas then omit the cold tea as there will be sufficient tannin in the skin of the dried grape.

CRANBERRY OR WORCESTERBERRY WINES

2 lb (1 kg) cranberries or worcesterberries
2½ lb (1.5 kg) sugar
1 lb (0.5 kg) sultanas
pectic enzyme
yeast

Cover the fruit with water in a saucepan and bring to the boil taking care not to overheat. Overheating will caramelise the natural sugars. Pour the liquid and the fruit on to the minced sultanas and sugar contained in a fermenting bucket. Stir thoroughly and add a further three pints (1.5 litres) of cold water. When the temperature is 70°F (21°C) add the yeast and pectic enzyme. After a week strain, transfer to a demijohn and ferment in the usual way.

Sweet worcesterberry wine should be made by the method given for gooseberry, page 94.

OTHER BERRY WINES

Virtually any berry fruit that you know is not poisonous may be used for winemaking. Amongst the best known are barberries, berberis and fuchsia. Such berry fruits may be converted to wine by the following general method. The quality of the wine will depend very much on which berries are used.

2 lb (1 kg) berries
2½ lb (1.25 kg) sugar
1 lb (0.5 kg) sultanas
1 tsp citric acid
pectic enzyme
yeast

Remove the berries from the stalks and place together with the minced sultanas and sugar in the fermentation bucket. Cover with six pints (3 litres) of boiling water. Allow the liquid to cool to 70°F (21°C) and add the yeast and enzyme. Stir daily. When the initial head has subsided, strain, transfer to a demijohn, top up with water and fit an air lock.

Variation
A wine made to this recipe will be medium dry, for a sweeter wine use an extra half pound (250 gm) of sugar.

Should you find that your wine is thin, then incorporate the liquid obtained from boiling one pound (0.5 kg) of bananas in half a pint (250 ml) of water for twenty minutes in the brew.

Providing that the wine is not harsh — a sign of an over predominance of acid or tannin — you may in future brews increase the quantity of berries to four pounds (2 kg).

BLOOD PLUMS AND LOQUATS

Wine from these two fruits, indigenous to Australia, should be made as described under greengage.

MELON WINE

Novelty wines can be made from all melons, including honeydew, sugar, water and rock melons. Make the wine by the method given for marrow or pumpkin wine, using six pounds (3.0 kg) of melon.

TROPICAL FRUIT WINE

Avocado pears, custard apples, guavas, lychees, mangos, paw paws, passion fruit (and banana passion fruit), persimmons and pineapples all make very enjoyable wines. Once the fruit is prepared, the wines are all made in the same way and may be considered together.

3 lb (1.5 kg) fruit, if using pineapple 1 large one
2½ lb (1.25 kg) sugar for a dry wine or
3 lb (1.5 kg) sugar for a sweet wine
½ can of grape juice concentrate or
1 lb (0.5 kg) sultanas
1½ tsp citric acid
1 cup cold tea (omit if using sultanas)
pectic enzyme
yeast

Avocado pears, custard apples and paw paws should be skinned and cut up. Guavas should be washed and mashed. It is not practical to skin and remove the pips. Mangos and persimmons should also be washed and mashed. Passion fruit should be cut in half and flesh scooped out. Pineapples should be peeled and diced.

Place the prepared fruit in a bucket with the sugar and cover with four pints (2 litres) of boiling water. Stir thoroughly to dissolve the sugar, mashing the fruit in the process. Allow to cool, add the grape concentrate, citric acid, yeast, cold tea and pectic enzyme. If you are using minced sultanas, place these with the fruit and the sugar in the fermenting bucket. Cover with five pints (2.5 litres) of boiling water, allow to cool, add the other ingredients omitting the cold tea. Stir the wine daily, breaking up the fruit as much as possible. When the voluminous head has subsided, strain the juice into a demijohn, top up with tap water and finish in the usual manner.

FIG WINE

Next to grapes, figs are the best ingredient for making wines and if you have access to a supply of fresh figs then you should make some wine from them.

4 lb (2 kg) fresh figs
2 lb (1 kg) sugar
pectic enzyme
yeast

Cut up the figs and add them to the sugar in the fermenting vessel. Cover with six pints (3 litres) of boiling water. When the mix is cool enough to handle, stir thoroughly to dissolve the sugar. After a week strain and ferment to dryness.

If you prefer a sweeter wine use an extra pound (0.5 kg) of figs and an extra half pound (250 gm) of sugar.

You can make a sweet sherry type wine from figs. Oxidise the sweeter wine as described under parsnip and add one tablespoonful of glycerine per bottle. In temperate regions it is better to use dried figs according to the recipe given for dried apricots (November) replacing the apricots with an equal weight of figs.

NOVELTY WINE

Recipes have been given for most of the more popular winemaking ingredients of Britain, North America, Australia and New Zealand, but this is by no means the complete range of possibilities. Other wines that are not as popular as those discussed — but in many instances are still worth making for their novelty value — can be produced by simply adapting the standard recipes.

CEREAL WINES

In addition to wheat wine, barley wine — not the type containing hops which is a beer — and maize wine are also popular. Make sure that the cereal is fit for human consumption, some animal grade feedstuffs are not.

Crush the grain and make the wine according to the method given for wheat wine.

FLOWER WINES

There are many different flowers throughout the British Isles and abroad whose fragrant perfumes would make them ideally suited to winemaking. However country wine making evolved centuries ago, when the only flowers to experiment with were those native to these shores and consequently there is no information available about those multitude of species which have been introduced during the last one or two centuries, or the many hybrids which are now available. It is the danger of using a poisonous flower, which stops wholesale experimentation in what must surely be one of the richest new sources of winemaking ingredient.

Only if you know that a flower head is not poisonous should you entertain using it for winemaking. Always remove all trace of greenery which will give the wine a bitter taste, then using a half pint (250 ml) of lightly fragrant bloom or a quarter of a pint (125 ml) of a strongly scented flower to make a gallon (4.5 litres) of wine, use any of the recipes described to make flower wines under April, where this style of drink is extensively discussed.

HERB WINES

On top of the herb wines for which recipes have already been given there are those which are made by herb infusion into a standard wine.

Two ounces (50 gm) of the fresh herb, or half that quantity of dried material is usually sufficient. You can always use more (or less) when you make the wine again — but remember that most herbs are strongly flavoured. Amongst the herbs you might like to try are sage, rosemary, mint, hops, thyme and marjoram.

2 oz (50 gm) fresh herbs
or 1 oz (25 gm) dried herbs
1 lb (0.5 kg) minced sultanas or raisins
2 tsp citric acid
pectic enzyme
yeast

Place the minced sultanas or raisins and the sugar in the fermentation vessel and cover with one gallon (4.5 litres) of boiling water. Place the herbs in a muslin bag, to which a piece of string has been attached and suspend it in the bucket for two hours. Remove the herbs, if they are left longer the flavour will be overpowering. Add the yeast and the enzyme and finish the wine in the usual manner.

ARTIFICIAL FLAVOURED WINES

If the base wine above, without the herbs, is made, then by using a dropper and adding flavouring to the bottle a whole range of 'artificial wines' can be produced. Try orange, lemon, cherry, raspberry, strawberry, mint and sherry flavouring.

SAP WINES

Maple sap wine is one of the great country wines of North America. This wine can be made in the same way as birch sap wine, but since maple syrup contains its own fermentable sugars reduce the amount of added sugar to two pounds (1 kg). Sycamore and walnut saps are also used for wine making and these again should be made by the birch sap method and with the same quantities. See March wines for details.

VEGETABLE WINES

If you consult the winemaking literature you will find recipes for virtually every known vegetable, but even I draw the line at cabbage wine. Some of the more interesting vegetable wines are:

TOMATO WINE

4 lb (2 kg) tomato
3 lb (1.5 kg) sugar
1 tsp citric acid
yeast

This is a very simple wine to make. Cut the tomatoes into quarters, place in the fermenting vessel together with the sugar. Cover with boiling water and when cool add the yeast and maintain at 70°F (21°C). Strain the liquid into a demijohn after a week and ferment to dryness.

RUNNER OR FRENCH BEAN WINE

Runner or French beans, like pea pods, give body to a wine and can be incorporated in virtually any fruit wine recipe. Simply wash the beans, slice and add to the fruit, in place of the sultanas, prior to covering with the boiling water. Alternatively, a very cheap wine can be made from runner or French beans, using the recipe given for pea pod replacing the pea pods with two pounds (1 kg) of beans.

ROOT WINES

Mangolds can be used for winemaking. Employ the recipe given for carrot wine, replacing the carrots with four pounds (2 kg) of the root. Celeriac is a fairly strongly flavoured vegetable, so to make a wine from this root use only two pounds (1 kg) of it, but again use the carrot method.

CELERY WINE

Some people enjoy the flavour of celery in a country wine and this can be produced by the method given for lettuce. Simply replace the lettuce with one head of celery.

FRUIT WINES

It is impossible to give a recipe for every type of fruit in the world, but you can produce your own recipe if you are prepared for a little trial and error. If you use the method given below to make your first gallon (4.5 litres) it will be drinkable, probably very enjoyable, but if, based on the experience of your first brew, you adjust the ingredients then you will be able to make yet another wine to your personal taste.

Take two pounds (1 kg) of strongly flavoured fruit or four pounds (2 kg) of one with a delicate flavour, peel or remove the skin and if possible remove the seeds. Place in a bucket with one pound (0.5 kg) of minced sultanas and two and a half pounds (1.25 kg) sugar and cover with six pints (3 litres) of boiling water. If this does not provide a gallon (4.5 litres) of liquid, it can always be made up with tap water when the liquid is transferred to a demijohn.

If the fruit tastes very sweet, do not add any extra acid if using four pounds (2 kg) of fruit; if you only use two pounds (1 kg) add one teaspoonful of citric acid. If the fruit lacks an acid taste, add two teaspoonfuls of citric acid to two pounds (1 kg) of fruit or half the quantity to four pounds (2 kg). Alternatively you can use an acid testing kit and determine scientifically the amount of acid that is required. Add yeast and pectic enzyme at 70°F (21°C) and ferment the wine as described earlier in the text.

It is possible to make an infinite number of fruit wines by mixing together different fruit. Since the fruits will each contribute their own flavour the net effect often, but not always, is an improvement in the quality of the wine.

Remember also to incorporate the juice of bananas, to try replacing sultanas with crushed wheat and to blend the finished wines. Obviously there is no limit to the scope in country wine making; the recipes included in the calendar were originally produced according to these principles, tested, adjusted and retested. Whilst these are the best wines I have to date managed to make, there is no reason why you should not make better wines, either from the most popular ingredients, or from some lesser known fruits. If there is one thing that is guaranteed to give you more satisfaction than making a good wine from one of my recipes it will be making a good wine from your own recipe.

CANNED FRUIT AND FRUIT JUICES

These have become very popular for making wines in recent years and they produce very good wines in the minimum period of time and with the least effort. However they do have the disadvantage that the wine tends to be slightly more expensive than that made from fresh fruit. The recipes given in the calendar, under February, are for those fruit that are not usually available at a more economic price for winemaking. You can, however, use any canned fruit replacing that given in the recipe with a can of equal weight of your own choice. This almost invariably produces a superb table wine.

Similarly wines can be made from juices other than those given in the February recipe, but here the choice is considerably less as there are few fruit juices, compared to canned fruits, on the market. Under no circumstances make wine from fruit squashes since these contain preservatives which stop them fermenting in the bottle. These preservatives make them unsuitable for winemaking.

GRAPE JUICE CONCENTRATE

So popular has home winemaking become that it is now possible to buy a whole range of grape juice concentrates. These are made by removing the water from natural grape juice by evaporation under reduced pressure, and the theory is that all the home vintner has to do is to reconstitute the liquid by adding water and this liquid will be similar to that employed to make the world's greatest wines. Whilst some of the concentrates are very good, the home winemaker — who invariably receives some cans as presents — is often disappointed with the result.

Any grape juice concentrates that you receive are best used in recipes where this is given as an ingredient. Should you wish to make a wine simply from the concentrate and one other ingredient, ignore any additives such as sugar and acid that the manufacturer recommends and add instead one pound (0.5 kg) of canned blackberries to a red concentrate or one pound (0.5 kg) of canned gooseberries to a white concentrate. The resulting wine will be far superior to that made just from the concentrate and will usually bear a close resemblance to commercial red or white wine.

POISONOUS PLANTS

Most fruits and plant materials are safe for winemaking but there are some which are poisonous. It is not possible to give a complete list of plants which are unsuitable for winemaking as there is insufficient knowledge of the subject. Plants which do not cause fatalities may cause stomach upsets and therefore never attempt to make a wine unless you know that the ingredients are safe to use. Plants which are known to be dangerous include American currant (ornamental variety), deadly nightshade, holly, honeysuckle (the berries, but not the flowers), mistletoe, privet and yew. However, this list must not be considered as being complete.

T·H·E F·I·N·I·S·H·E·D W·I·N·E

Wines vary considerably from season to season and individual palates differ — do not worry if your tastes are not similar to the 'experts', the wine that you like best is the best wine for you to make — consequently you may like to alter the characteristics of your wine after fermentation has ceased.

If you can identify the improvement that you wish to make and you possess several gallons of wine, this is best done by blending. Only blend wines of similar quality. Blending two single gallons (4.5 litres) of good wine can result in two gallons (9 litres) of great wine; blending two lower grade wines will result in something far more acceptable than either on their own. But if you blend a good quality wine with one of a poorer quality then all that you are likely to get is two gallons (9litres) of inferior wine, effectively losing the quality of the better. The art of blending, the true skill of the winemaker, will only come with experience and is best done first on small sample quantities with frequent tasting. Sometimes blending equal volumes of wines does not give the best results so do not be frightened to use other combinations, such as two parts of one wine with one of another, or to experiment with blending three or four different wines.

Where only slight corrections are necessary, then a slight addition to the finished wine is all that is required. The more common faults of balance and their identification are given below.

ACIDITY

A wine lacking in acidity will be bland and lifeless. For immediate drinking, extra lactic acid, which is far mellower than other types of acid and does not give a characteristic lemon taste, should be added to the wine. Dissolve a level teaspoonful in the minimum amount of water and add half of this to the gallon (4.5 litres) of wine. Alternatively you may add direct to the bottled wine, in which case dilute the solution further so that you can add one twelfth of a teaspoonful to the bottle. But do not dilute the solution too much as you do not want to make your wine any weaker than is absolutely necessary. Further additions of the acid solution, to taste, should be made until the correct level is reached.

If you cannot obtain lactic acid, you may add citric acid, but you will have to keep the wine at least a month, preferably longer, before drinking.

Wines containing only a slight excess of acid, will mellow on standing — it is a sign of a well made wine if, whilst it is still young, it is slightly harsh due to an excess of acid and tannin.

Should the wine still contain an excess of acid after about six months, and there is no sign of this acidity disappearing, then it should be blended with a wine low in this ingredient. This is always a far better alternative than any chemical method of removing acidity.

ALCOHOL

The only time, apart from when making liqueurs, that the home winemaker should consider fortifying a wine is if he wishes to make either a sherry or port type. Otherwise the expense defeats one of the major objects of home winemaking. For this reason only wines that are already high in alcohol should be fortified. Addition of two fluid ounces (50 ml) of 65 per cent proof brandy or vodka — no other spirit should be used as it will impart its own flavour to the wine — will raise the alcohol level of a bottle of a 16 per cent wine by a further 2 per cent. This will give it a similar strength to that of commercial ports and sherries. To ascertain whether a wine is high in alcohol, take a small quantity of the wine in the mouth, and without swallowing, suck air into the throat. The more intense the burning sensation the stronger the wine. You cannot determine the amount of alcohol present in all wines simply by swallowing, because some ingredients such as ginger give a similar sensation at the back of the throat.

BODY

Wines that lack body are thin to the taste and the absence of the buffering effect that body produces results in all imperfections of the wine being readily apparent. If a wine lacks body, one or even two tablespoonfuls of glycerine may be added. Glycerine has a slight sweetening effect on the wine and should not be used in excess. Shake thoroughly and allow to stand at least a month before drinking. Wines that appear to possess too much body require sweetening.

SWEETNESS

Wines that are not sufficiently sweet may be sweetened by the addition of sugar syrup or solid sugar. Shake thoroughly and taste carefully between each addition. Whilst the sugar will take some time to mix completely, wines treated in this manner should not be kept for long periods as refermentation may occur. This problem may be overcome by using lactose, available from all homebrew shops, which is virtually non-fermentable sugar. Lactose is less sweet than sugar and larger quantities must be used.

Non-fermentable sweeteners such as saccharin tend to give the wine an unacceptable taste and are best avoided.

TANNIN

The novice winemaker finds great difficulty in distinguishing between a lack (or excess) of acid and tannin. Excess tannin is noticed as a harshness on the gums and cheeks, whereas acid gives a similar sensation at the back of the throat. A lack of tannin, like acid, results in a bland wine. Treat by dropwise addition of grape tannin solution to the bottle. Wines so treated are ready for drinking immediately.

Where there is a slight excess of tannin, which is the cause of harshness in a wine, this disappears with maturation. This problem occurs with poorly prepared elderberry wines, and it is better to keep them rather than try to cure the problem by blending.

STORAGE OF WINES

'The older the wine, the better the taste' is a common, yet not always true belief. Certainly some wines, including all desserts and a few red table wines, are not at their best for drinking until they are at least two years old and they still go on improving for several years. But the vast majority of wines are well worth drinking after six months and some wines such as light white table wines that are not high in alcohol, sugar and tannin — all of which are necessary for the keeping of a wine — actually begin to deteriorate after about eighteen months.

All wines soon deteriorate if they are not stored under suitable conditions and the successful winemaker is as meticulous about the storage of his wine as he is about the manner in which the fermentation is conducted.

Racking and clarification of the wine must be completed before it is stored. Any sediment will rapidly decay, causing the wine to develop irreversible off flavours. Equally important is to ensure that the air gap between the top of the liquid and the cork is no more than one inch (2.5 cm). Excess oxygen also produces strong off flavours, in some instances very rapidly. But it is necessary to have a small amount of air present to allow certain desirable chemical reactions, which are responsible for much of the maturation process, to occur.

Wine can either be stored in bulk in demijohns or in bottles; one gallon (4.5 litres) of wine will fill six twenty-six fluid ounce (70 cl) bottles. The latter method is preferable if you do not possess a large quantity of wine, for not only does it release demijohns for further winemaking, but you may open a bottle to see how the wine is maturing.

Before drinking the wine you must bottle it, never pour straight from a demijohn since the air that enters will destroy the wine before the whole gallon has been consumed.

Country winemakers in general do not treat their product with sufficient respect, placing their wines in any bottles that are available and seldom bothering to fix a label. Red and rosé wines should always be stored in dark bottles as light induces a reaction in the wine which destroys the delicate pigments, resulting in the wine acquiring a light brown appearance. From pure aesthetics it is difficult to improve upon the tall dark bottles used for many German wines for serving white table wines.

A little effort in selecting the correct bottle — if in doubt choose one used for selling a similar type of wine — a restaurant or winebar will provide you with all that you require, and the correct labelling, for just a few pence it is possible to buy labels and collars specially designed for the home winemaker which will reflect the care that you have taken in its preparation and put the drinker in the correct frame of mind to appreciate the wine. It should never be forgotten that wine is drunk with the eyes long before it reaches the lips.

Corks are a potential source of infection and should always be soaked overnight in a solution made from a Campden tablet and a pinch of citric acid in half a pint (250 ml) of water, prior to use. Either insert the corks with a flogger or invest in a corking machine. Cover with a plastic cap, this cap will not only complete the appearance of the bottle, but it will also help to stop infections entering via the cork which is not impervious to air.

It may be difficult to provide the ideal storage temperature of a constant 45°F (7°C). Space usually dictates where the wine is kept. Try to avoid extremes of temperature; do not stand bottles next to central heating radiators, and under no circumstances keep the wine in direct sunlight which can cause rapid deterioration. Lower temperatures than the ideal tend to present less of a problem than higher temperatures and spare rooms and garages make ideal storage areas. But do not allow the wine to freeze. Wine racks, apart from their pleasant appearance, are better for storing bottles than placing them on the floor. Laying a bottle on its side keeps the cork moist and swollen which minimises the danger of an excess of air entering the wine.

A simple wine rack can be constructed by making two identical wooden meshes made of slats four inches (10 cm) apart; you can make the racks as large as you like, but units to hold twenty-four bottles are most convenient. Place the second mesh four inches (10 cm) in front of the first and join at the four corners with a piece of wood one inch by one inch (2.5 cm × 2.5 cm).

Country wines are served in the same way as all wines: whites and rosés slightly chilled, and red wines at room temperature. No wine irrespective of its colour is at its best unless it is allowed to breathe prior to serving. And, contrary to general opinion, all wines, including whites, benefit from being uncorked two hours before serving, although this is not always possible.

WINES FOR COOKING

Wines greatly improve many dishes, but as a result of the cooking process and the marrying together of the flavour with that of the food, many of the finest characteristics of the wine are lost. Consequently only the cheaper ones are used for culinary purposes. It is the acid in the wine breaking down the tough protein which improves the texture of the meat, whilst the flavour marries with that of the meat itself yielding a dish superior to that prepared without wine.

Country wines are every bit as good in the kitchen as those bought, providing you choose those which are not too highly flavoured and bear the closest resemblance to commercial wines. Where a recipe calls for a red wine, use a dry elderberry, blackberry or bilberry. The best white wines for culinary purposes are apple, citrus fruit and flower wines. Parsnip wine is an excellent substitute for sherry and greatly improves the quality of Christmas puddings.

If you have not tried wine in your cookery, begin by simply adding a glass when you make the gravy and sit back and wait for the compliments.

FAULTS IN WINEMAKING

Providing you take precautions with your sterilisation and maintain the correct conditions for the yeast, then faults in your wine will be extremely rare. Nevertheless they do occasionally occur, and depending upon how quickly they are spotted, the wine can often be saved.

Acetification or Vinegaring of the Wine

This results from the airborne spores of the vinegar yeast entering the wine at some stage of its preparation or maturation. Generally it is best to throw the wine away as no treatment is effective. Should you be able to tolerate a small degree of vinegaring, drink the wine immediately you detect the taste as it will rapidly get worse.

Cattiness

Very occasionally elder wines, either flower or berry, exhibit a bouquet reminiscent of cats. Those elder bushes prone to the problem, the cause of which is not fully understood, have a catty smell about them especially when in flower and should be avoided.

Cloudiness

Should the wine fail to clear, provided that the trouble is not the result of either a pectin or starch haze, the wine can usually be cleared by treatment with Bentonite.

Prepare the Bentonite by placing a level teaspoonful of the insoluble powder, or the gel which is better, in a cup full of wine and mix thoroughly. Divide the wine into two by placing half in a second demijohn and add equal amounts of the Bentonite paste and liquid to each demijohn and shake for ten minutes. After shaking, recombine the liquid and allow to stand for a week. If the wine is still not clear add wine finings which are often very effective. Should a haze still be present it will probably be due to pectin or starch, depending upon what ingredients were used. You might try adding the appropriate enzyme, if you did not include it in the initial preparation, but this is not always effective at this late stage in the wine's life.

Don't be in too much of a hurry to artificially clear the wine, they often clear as a result of reaction by chemicals already present in the liquid simply on standing.

Flowers of Wine

This is the name given to a white film appearing on the top of a wine and is due to an infection by spoilage yeasts. These live on alcohol and break it down to carbon dioxide. Treat the wine with the addition of one crushed Campden tablet per gallon (4.5 litres). The wine will not have very good keeping qualities, due to the loss of alcohol and should be drunk as soon as the taste of sulphite has disappeared.

Medicinal Taste

This is the consequence of insufficient or no acid in the must. Any wine showing this defect cannot be saved. If acid is included in the recipe add an extra teaspoonful; where no acid was used employ twice this amount next time you make this particular brew.

Mousiness

Sometimes a wine has a distinct mouse-like bouquet and a taste to match. If the taste is only slight, the wine can often be saved by the addition of a Campden tablet to each gallon (4.5 litres) of wine.

Where a slight mousy taste occurs with reds such as elderberries, this is due to the ingredients. Allowing the wine to breathe before serving usually cures the problem.

Mustiness

Wines that have been allowed to stand on the sediment of dead yeast cells, termed the lees, result in the development of a musty taste. Allowing the wine to breathe sometimes helps, but if the wine is too musty it is best destroyed.

Oiliness or Ropiness

The appearance of a layer of oil or rope-like threads in the wine is a result of infection by bacteria. The wine should be treated as for flowers of wine.

Oxidation

If a wine that has stood for any period of time in a half filled container has an off flavour it will probably be due to excessive oxidation. Treatment with one or two Campden tablets, depending upon how strong the flavour is, will go some way towards reversing the process. Beware — never drink much of an excessively oxidised wine as it can give you a very bad headache and hangover.

Stuck Ferments

Before you decide that a ferment has stuck, that is ceased working prematurely, check by taste or with an hydrometer that the wine is not dry.

Where fermentable sugar is still present and you know from the quantity added that there is less than 16 per cent alcohol present then the wine should be restarted. As there will be some alcohol present, it may be more difficult to restart than to establish the initial fermentation.

Check that the temperature is correct, if you did not add nutrient initially then add it before attempting to restart the must. But if you have already added nutrient, do not add it again as an excess may affect the taste of the wine. Add a fresh, vigorously working starter. If this does not cure the problem, place half the wine in a second demijohn fitted with an airlock. Shake both demijohns to dissolve some of the oxygen in the air, then add a yeast starter to both batches of wine. When the fermentation is proceeding again, usually after two or three days, recombine the two portions in one demijohn.

Stuck ferments may be restarted simply by racking when the small quantity of air dissolved is sufficient to allow the yeast to commence an aerobic phase which results in a build up of the number of cells present.

Sulphite

Excess taste and bouquet of sulphite due to treatment with either Campden tablets or sodium metabisulphite will disappear with keeping. Should this objectionable taste persevere for longer than usual, allow the wine to breathe for a few hours and it will disappear.

EXHIBITING WINES

Exhibiting wines is becoming increasingly popular and nowadays most horticultural societies include wine making classes in their shows. By entering your wines you not only stand a chance of winning prizes (many of the recipes included in this book have won me first prizes and cups) but if you ask the judge afterwards he will give you an honest opinion and you will learn a great deal about your wines.

Before showing, consult the schedule carefully for special presentation regulations, failure to comply with these can result in disqualification. If no instructions are given, exhibit the wine in a Sauterne type bottle. These are made of clear glass, with shoulders and a punt. Use an all cork stopper and if no instructions are given place a 2 × ¾ inch (5 × 2 cm) label one inch (2.5 cm) from the base and midway between the seams of the bottle. Write the class number and the name of the main ingredient on the label. If you are not sure in which class to enter a particular wine ask the secretary, who will be pleased to give you the relevant details.

When preparing wines for show, prepare two bottles of the same wine a week before. Because wines sometimes start to throw a sediment after rebottling, decant the top half of both bottles into a third. The bottle used for the actual showing should be absolutely clean and this can only be achieved by washing in hot soapy water.

The wine that will win prizes is the one that is properly presented, in the correct bottle with the right label and cork. The wine should have a brilliant appearance but above all a pleasing flavour and bouquet.

WINE CIRCLES

Wine circles, providing a wide range of lectures and social activities, started in England and several exist in many towns in this country and abroad. If you would like to join a circle, and membership is usually very cheap, you will be made most welcome, winemakers are very gregarious. Details of local clubs can be found in most public libraries.

G·L·O·S·S·A·R·Y O·F
W·I·N·E·M·A·K·I·N·G T·E·R·M·S

Winemaking has evolved its own vocabulary which is often confusing to the beginner. Some of the more commonly employed terms are briefly explained below. Where necessary a more detailed description is given in the text.

ACETALDEHYDE   The first oxidation product of alcohol, responsible for much of the character of sherries.

ACETIC ACID   The harsh acid found in vinegar.

ACETIFICATION   The conversion of wine to vinegar as a result of bad winemaking.

AEROBIC FERMENTATION   Fermentation conducted in the presence of excess air.

ALCOHOL   A class of organic compounds — in winemaking taken to mean ethanol (ethyl alcohol).

AMYLASE   An enzyme added mainly to root vegetables and cereals to destroy starch.

AMMONIUM PHOSPHATE   A compound that provides important yeast nutrients.

ANAEROBIC FERMENTATION   Fermentation conducted in the absence of air.

APERITIF   A wine for drinking before a meal to stimulate the appetite. Vermouths and dry sherries are the best known commercial aperitifs.

B1   Vitamin essential for the development of yeast.

BALANCE   The relationship between the various components of the wine.

BEAD   Bubbles of carbon dioxide, seen in the glass when sparkling wine is served.

BENTONITE   Naturally occurring clay used to clear wines.

BLAND   Used to describe an insipid wine which lacks acid, tannin, alcohol or all three.

BODY   The weight or thickness of a wine, lack of it results in a thin wine.

BOUQUET   The aroma of the wine.

BRILLIANCE   Describes the highest degree of clarity.

CAMPDEN TABLETS   Sterilising and reducing agent, mainly sodium metabisulphite, but often containing other stabilising chemicals such as sodium benzoate.

CARBON DIOXIDE (CO₂)   A gas consisting of one part carbon and two parts oxygen released during fermentation.

CHAPTALISATION   Addition of sugar to grape juice to supplement that naturally present.

CITRIC ACID   Acid found in lemons.

CLARITY   The absence or presence of suspended solids.

CLOUDINESS   Suspension of insoluble particles in the liquid.

CYSER   Ferment of apple juice and honey.

DECANTING   Pouring clear wine from sediment formed during maturation.

DEMIJOHN   Fermenting vessel.

DESSERT WINE   The fullest and sweetest of all wines.

DISTILLATION   The process of separating alcohol from water. Dangerous and in most countries, illegal.

ENZYMES   Biologically produced compounds that bring about chemical reactions.

FAREWELL   The taste remaining in the mouth after drinking a wine.

FERMENTATION   The metabolism of yeast produces alcohol

FERMENTING TO DRYNESS   The converting of all available sugar to alcohol.

FILTRATION   Physical separation of suspended particles to aid clarification.

FINING   Chemical treatment of a wine to aid clarification.

FORTIFICATION   Addition of alcohol to increase the strength of a wine.

FRUCTOSE   Sugar found in most fruit, produced from sucrose by inversion.

GERANIUM   Off flavour similar to that of a geranium, formed as a result of treating a wine with potassium sorbate without the addition of a Campden tablet.

GLUCOSE   Sugar obtained from sucrose as a result of inversion.

GLYCERINE   Compound responsible for much of the natural body of a wine. Can be artificially added in small quantities.

GOLDEN   Colour of a wine, golden wines should show no sign of browning as a result of oxidation.

GREEN   Used to describe young wine which possesses a sharp taste due to the immaturity of the acids.

HARSH   A wine containing too much acid or tannin.

HAZE   The presence of minute particles, usually due to starch or pectin, that cannot be removed by fining or filtering.

HIPPOCRAS   Spiced pyment.

INITIAL FERMENTATION   The stage at which the yeast breeds.

INSTANT WINES   Wines ready for drinking in three to six weeks.

INVERSION   The process of converting sucrose to glucose and fructose.

INVERTASE   The enzyme responsible for the inversion of sugar.

INVERT SUGAR   A mixture of equal amounts of fructose and glucose.

LACTIC ACID   The mellowest of all acids, derived from milk.

LACTOSE   Sugar derived from milk, virtually unfermentable.

LEES   Sediment or dead yeast and fruit cells formed during fermentation.

MADERISATION   The development of a caramel-like flavour, similar to that found in madeira, in a wine. The result of using raisins or oxidation of the wine.

MAGNESIUM SULPHATE   Epsom salts, a useful nutrient.

MALIC ACID   Naturally occurring acid found in grapes, apples and other fruits.

MALOLACTIC FERMENTATION   Occasionally occurring third stage of fermentation resulting in the conversion of malic into lactic acid.

MATURATION   The ageing of the wine.

MELOMEL   A ferment of honey and any fruit juice.

METHYL ALCOHOL (METHANOL)   Woodspirit, it is a highly poisonous alcohol, can be produced from wild yeasts and as a result of poor winemaking technique, but it is generally not a problem.

MOUSINESS   The bouquet and flavour similar to the smell of mice, found in some affected wines.

MUST   The liquid and fruit from which wine is made.

MUSTINESS   Mouldy taste due to leaving the wine too long on the lees.

NUTRIENTS   Compound other than sugar and acids essential to the yeast's development.

OXALIC ACID   Poisonous acid found in rhubarb and certain other plants, but presents no problems if the musts are treated as described.

OXIDATION   Any chemical process in which compounds react with the oxygen of the air.

PECTIC ENZYME   Sold under a variety of trade names, it is an enzyme that destroys pectin.

PECTIN   Natural compound found in fruit after boiling. It is responsible for the setting of jams and causes hazes in wines.

PROOF   An old standard (still used for spirits) of quoting the alcoholic strength of wines. 100° proof is equal to 57.1 per cent alcohol.

PUNT   Large indentation in the base of a wine bottle.

PYMENT   Any ferment of grape juice and honey.

RACKING Separation of the wine from the lees by syphoning.

REDUCTION Any process by which oxygen is lost from a compound; the reverse of oxidation.

ROSÉ A delicate table wine that has a pale pink colour.

SECONDARY FERMENTATION The anaerobic fermentation. Maximum conversion of sugar to alcohol occurs during this stage.

SOCIAL WINES Wine for general drinking rather than accompanying a meal, midway between a dessert and table wine in character.

SODIUM METABISULPHITE Compound that liberates sulphur dioxide on reaction with citric acid.

STARCH Non fermentable compound found in vegetables and cereals that can cause a haze in wines.

STARCH ENZYME See amylase.

STERILISATION The killing of micro-organisms.

STUCK FERMENT Premature cessation of fermentation.

SUCROSE Ordinary household sugar, derived from either cane or beet. The most suitable sugar for winemaking.

SULPHITE The taste of sulphur dioxide in a wine, or for sulphur dioxide in general.

SULPHUR DIOXIDE (SO$_2$) A gas consisting of one part sulphur and two parts oxygen liberated by either Campden tablets or sodium metabisulphite. A sterilising agent.

TABLE WINE The lightest of all wines, designed to be drunk with meals. Table wines should contain about 12 per cent alcohol.

TANNIN Compound found in the skins and stems of fruit that gives a harsh taste detected on the gums.

TARTARIC ACID The main acid of the grape.

TAWNY WINE Rich brown coloured dessert wine. The colour is a fault in lighter wines, whose balance cannot carry the oxidation necessary to produce this effect.

THIAMIN Vitamin B1.

THIN A wine lacking body.

VINEGAR A wine in which some of the alcohol has been converted by micro-organisms into acetic acid.

VINOSITY Wine-like character of the liquid.

WOODINESS A taste resulting from fermenting hard fruits in the presence of their stones, or blackberries in the presence of their pips.

YEAST Micro-organisms that convert sugar into alcohol.

ZYMASE An enzyme involved in the conversion of sugar into alcohol.

I·N·D·E·X